God Is at the Meeting

Dear John,
When it comes to
the 12 steps, I know
enough to be dangerous.
I'm sure you've read &
heard much of this before,
but I hope you find it
useful   Be well!
                Scooter
                1/31/13

God Is at the Meeting

Meeting

Spirituality and the Twelve Steps

Maurice C.

WestBow
PRESS
A DIVISION OF THOMAS NELSON

WestBow Press books may be ordered through booksellers or by contacting:

WestBow Press
A Division of Thomas Nelson
1663 Liberty Drive
Bloomington, IN 47403
www.westbowpress.com
1-(866) 928-1240

ISBN: 978-1-4497-2622-5 (e)
ISBN: 978-1-4497-2623-2 (sc)
ISBN: 978-1-4497-2624-9 (hc)

Library of Congress Control Number: 2011915521

Printed in the United States of America

WestBow Press rev. date: 10/18/2011

Contents

Dedication

This book is dedicated to all my brothers and sisters who suffer from alcohol addiction, especially those who are incarcerated. I have learned a vast amount about our disease from Alcoholics Anonymous (AA) meetings and from visits to jails and prisons. My purpose in writing this book is to relate real experiences of men and women who have recovered and to suggest that the AA way of life is available to anyone who wants it. The stories are true. I have frequently changed the names to protect the guilty. The anecdotes come from people who reach that point in their addiction where they finally called out for help. These notes are written to support all of us who have surrendered to our addiction as we attempt to better understand the spiritual solution to that addiction while standing firm with the Power who provides the solution.

Over the years, I have been blessed to be called "sponsor" by some wonderful men. Their confiding in me has humbled me, and their love and consideration of the few words I offered them is a gift immeasurable. Working with them has kept my nose in the AA literature and my feet on the right path for a lot of years. It is an honor to walk through life with these men; I love them and thank them for all the blessings they have brought into my life. While I have worked with these men, I have no power to confer sobriety on them. In AA, we all have the opportunity to share the Higher Power, the author of sobriety, with our fellows. The alcoholic has to take hold of the opportunity. Sponsors take the small steps as God's messenger, and He does the work.

I want to thank the men at the Thursday-evening meeting "The Last Man Standing" at the Wynne Unit in Huntsville,

Maurice C.

Texas. Their encouragement kept me going when I doubted the value of this effort. In addition, I need to thank Claudia Amen for her proofreading and Cheri Tillman for her many hours of editing my wandering words. Both of these women were employed with me during my first days in AA and were good enough not to shoot me back then. They worked with me for almost twenty years, and after all that, were still willing to volunteer their time to help me with this book.

Most importantly, I want to say thank you to my wife and children, who suffered the most from the insanity of my addiction. I thank them for their patience, encouragement, and support. I love them and respect them. By trying to live the principles of AA, I am better able to love and serve them today. I will never be able to take back all the harm and discomfort I brought to my family. The only thing I can do is make daily amends by living the life God has given me through AA. My sons have taught me how to be a father. They have been, and are, loving and generous. I am proud of them and who they have become without a lot of help from me. When I was a young father, my addiction interfered with my ability to love them unconditionally. I didn't fully understand the meaning of unconditional love until my sons had children. Now I know the love of a grandparent for a grandchild can be unbelievably spontaneous and unconditional. I can only say thank you to my sons and their children for teaching me something I never knew or experienced as a child. My deepest thanks go to my wife, who, through the years of my addiction, kept our family together and is primarily responsible for raising our sons to be the men they are today.

Preface:
Spirituality in the Twelve Steps

Simply put, Alcoholics Anonymous (AA) saved my life. It can do the same for you.

Like many others addicted to alcohol, I was on the road to slowly killing myself while unwittingly hurting those around me, especially my family. Through a number of circumstances and with help from people I didn't even know, I found myself at the doors of my first AA meeting in 1985. Thank God, I have never left. We will talk more about the process of AA meetings and what you can expect in a later chapter, but suffice it to say that when I first went, I had little knowledge of AA or its practices. As time went by, I learned to do what was suggested to me: go to meetings, read the literature, get a sponsor, and learn and work the Twelve Steps. I laugh now when I remember thinking that AA would teach me how to either slow down or better handle my drinking. My life was going downhill fast and I was desperate to do something—anything—to stop the slide. I had reached my moment of clarity and asked for help.

I went to my first AA meeting thinking that if these people could show me how not to drink by some form of self-denial or discipline, I would go for it. As with most alcoholics, I believed the answer to my problem lay in me—what I had to do, what I would deny myself, or what discipline I could undertake. I was ready for a course in how not to drink, and I was greatly surprised that that was not the case at all.

By watching others in the program, coming to believe in the process, and truly listening to my fellows at meetings, aided by the grace of God, I did stop drinking. I thought that would be impossible, but it worked. It really did. I didn't think I could live without alcohol until I saw the program work for others.

As I learned the Steps, I had another pleasant shock—they made sense! Actually, they made a lot of common sense! The Twelfth Step, however, caught me off guard. While I had believed that AA would involve self-denial, tough discipline, and long days of "just saying no," the words of the Twelfth Step brought great relief. The Twelfth Step, found on page 60 of *Alcoholics Anonymous* (also referred to as the *Big Book*) says, "Having had a spiritual awakening as the result of these Steps, we tried to carry this message to alcoholics and to practice these principles in all our affairs." The idea of a spiritual solution took a great weight off my shoulders. I didn't have to do this by myself, and it wasn't going to be painful. I found that AA is not a program of discipline and self-denial; rather, it is a roadmap to a full life based on practical and proven spiritual facts. What I thought would be a "non-drinking" group turned out to be a wonderful, spiritually motivated group seeking sobriety by living a better life—a life where drinking and drugging are not necessary and where service to God and fellow man, especially other alcoholics, can be fun. In this AA crowd—a bunch of rummies, liars, thieves, and worse—I found a calling to a spiritual way of life.

So, how do we in AA define a "spiritual" way of life? The word spirituality is used so much today that it is hard to grasp its meaning. A good friend of mine recently told me that she doesn't even like the word because it has lost its meaning. It has become too Hollywoodish, with many in the celebrity universe saying that they are spiritual or seeking a spiritual path. They never define their path in a way I can understand. My observation is that if you have to go somewhere or get onto a plane or train to find spirituality, you are probably traveling too far.

People also frequently say that they are not "religious," they are "spiritual." This means, I suppose, that they don't need a religion to know God or live a spiritual life. My friend who dislikes the word spiritual believes they are just too lazy to figure out what they really believe. These folks learn about God in other settings rather than in a religious setting. I went to an internet search engine and to Webster's dictionary to find current definitions of spirituality. I think the founders of AA would be laughing out loud if they read what I found, especially at some of the politically correct explanations I found on the Internet. There is a concept of secular spirituality and even a concept of "green" spirituality, but I think that neither is what the AA founders were talking about. The spirituality of AA is based on Judeo-Christian thought and experience, but rather than getting involved in a debate, let's agree that the spirituality embodied in AA works for alcoholics and addicts—period. That is the operative principle, and it works—it really does.

Spirituality, as found in the AA literature and traditions, is simple to define, and it is alive in the Twelve Steps of AA. For me, AA spirituality is simply the effort to seek out and follow God's will rather than my own. The principles of AA move us from a self-serving life to a spiritual life of serving God and man. We learn to do this as we move through the Twelve Steps with the help of our sponsor and inspiration from our Higher Power. The concept of a Higher Power may be new to many and may cause some confusion. In its most simple form, the authors of the AA literature used the concept of Higher Power to mean simply a power greater than oneself. To avoid putting a roadblock in someone's mind, they never defined Higher Power as God, but it is always used with capital letters in the AA literature. My Higher Power is God.

If you are reading this book, it is probable that you are battling alcoholism or addiction or know someone who is. If you are the alcoholic, like most of us, you have probably tried beating your addiction on your own through your own power. Without help, the battle will continue for the rest of your life. It is like watching someone digging a ditch. Addicts are digging their way into the depths of alcohol and drug addiction. You can watch them day by day struggling and digging deeper and getting further away from sunlight. When an offer to help is presented, it is almost always rejected with, "I don't need your help. I don't want your help. I can do this on my own." Addicts dig deeper and deeper, rejecting every opportunity for help. Eventually they realize they can dig no further, or they keep digging until they die. Until they realize they need help and are willing to accept it, they are hopeless. If you are the one watching someone you love digging deeper and deeper, know that there is nothing you can do to magically cure him or her. When I was digging my hole with all my might, my wife tried to reach me. My response to her was, "Get off my back." All you can do is pray that they will reach out to the Power who can and will help them. Most of us in recovery had a loved one, parent, spouse, or child praying for us.

Through AA you will learn to become dependent upon a Power greater than yourself. God will do for you what you cannot do for yourself, and you will find that phrase used over and over in the AA literature. Ninety-nine percent of those of us in AA did not have the power within us to bring ourselves out of our addiction. Most of us tried to quit drinking or using, only to find ourselves back at the bottle, needle, or pill. We cannot overcome our addiction until we admit that no human power, either our own or that of another, can cure us. We have to learn to lean on a Power higher than our own. Once we find our Higher Power, a Power outside of ourselves, we learn to rely on that Power. The AA literature doesn't define Higher Power. That is up to each individual, but most of us come to believe that Higher Power is God and that His Power can and will relieve our addiction problems when we are willing to have Him work in our lives.

I know some readers might want to put the book down now—too much spiritual mumbo jumbo. Before you make that decision, read the words of the founders of AA in the *Big Book, Alcoholics Anonymous.* More than seventy-five years ago they wrote that neither you nor I are the center of the universe, nor are we a mystical participant in being God. While we believe God can and that God does live in us, we are not infinite, nor do we have godlike powers. He is our Creator and we are His not handiwork but works of art. It is not by looking into ourselves that we find God. Rather, by looking we find what separates us from God. We do have to look into ourselves, but the journey doesn't end there. In fact, it only begins there. Once we know who we are by performing the Twelve Steps of AA, we have the ability to understand who God is and how we can take a path to Him.

Explaining AA spirituality is one thing; living it is another. Rest assured you won't be asked to light candles, burn incense, sit in uncomfortable positions, or hold your thumb and forefinger together while sitting with your eyes closed and chanting. The spiritual life AA offers is very practical. It has to do with humility, self-sacrifice, and the surrender of self-will. It will take a new AA member awhile to figure that out, and that's a good thing. It comes slowly for most of us because we have spent many years thinking only of ourselves and how to make ourselves feel better through drink or drugs, no matter what the consequences. Spiritual living requires thinking more about and doing more for others than we do about and for ourselves. Knowledge of the spiritual life doesn't make us spiritual. Spirituality doesn't come from knowing the right chant, praying in the right place, learning from the right guru, or wearing an outward symbol. Internal transformation comes from our Higher Power and once we've accepted that Power the natural result will be spiritual living. The more we live the spiritual life, the closer we draw to the Higher Power and the closer we draw to the Higher Power, the more we want to live the spiritual life.

The people who make up AA demonstrate how the spirituality of the program has worked not only in their lives but also in the lives of thousands of others. These concepts work even though our efforts to live them are imperfect. Members have been uniquely blessed with access to spiritual living through the principles laid out for us by the founders of AA. Probably most of us would never have found the blessings of living a spiritual life if we were not alcoholic. In a strange way, then, we have access to a close connection to God that might never have happened if we hadn't sought to recover from our addiction. Stranger yet, many of us would never have had the opportunity to be so close to our Higher Power if we were not addicts. At many meetings you will hear someone say, "I am Mary. I am Joe. I am Pete. I am a grateful alcoholic." They are not grateful for the damage and harm done to themselves and others but grateful they have been given the gift of sobriety and knowledge of God they would never have known if not for membership in AA.

Esteem for the Conference-approved literature is paramount for all us who call ourselves members of Alcoholics Anonymous. If anything in this writing conflicts with or contradicts the words of our founders or our literature, rely on the real thing. Throughout this book, I will refer to the *Big Book, Alcoholics Anonymous* and to the Twelve by Twelve, which refers to the *Twelve Steps and Twelve Traditions*. At the end of each chapter in this book, there are suggested questions to ask yourself about the Step you just took. Hopefully the questions will encourage you to keep thinking through, and then living through, the Steps at an ever-deeper level. Each of us takes his own journey through AA. This book is my effort to share my experience in AA and how I came to understand spiritual living. I am neither a guru nor a circuit speaker, I am just a guy you might sit next to at a meeting; a guy who, like you, shares the blessings and joy of sobriety

Before moving on, read the words of an AA member. This man, a regular attendee at The Last Man Standing in the Wynne Unit, in Huntsville, Texas, shows how surrender to God can bring peace even in the most chaotic of places.

The Rose
By Raul M.

It's only a rose bud . . .
A flower of God's design;
But I cannot unfold the petals
With these clumsy hands of mine . . .

The secret of unfolding flowers
Is not known to such as I . . .
The flower God opens so sweetly
In my hands, would fade and die . . .

If I cannot unfold a rosebud,
This flower of God's design;
Then how can I think I have wisdom
To unfold this life of mine?

So . . . I'll trust in God for His leading
Each moment of every day,
And I'll look to God for His guidance
Each step of the way . . .

For the path that lies before me,
My Heavenly Father knows . . .
I'll trust God to unfold the moments
Just as He unfolds the rose.

How Did We Get into This Sorry Situation?

There is a wide range of addictions; but when a person becomes an addict, he or she has things in common with other addicts. Some common traits are an unfounded sense of shame and an insatiable need to build walls of self-protection resulting in a life of self-centeredness, where we put our needs above all others'.

These common traits are spread across the gamut of personalities and lifestyles. Some common traits are a sense of being alone, being insecure, a sense of inferiority or its opposite, superiority. Other common traits are anger, frustration, isolation, self-absorption, hypersensitivity, restlessness, irritability and discontentment. Sometimes the addiction is chalked up as hereditary, sometimes not. Some alcoholics and drug addicts live under bridges and sleep in the streets; some live in the best houses, travel in luxury and sleep in the finest hotels. It is not what's happening on the outside that is important, but what is going on on the inside. Alcoholism is no respecter of age, race, or economic status. The addiction can be just as virulent in the mansion as in the sewer. We tend to think of alcoholics as those men and women huddled on the sidewalk, chugging out of a bottle wrapped in a brown paper bag. The truth is, there are probably more alcoholics sitting in the corner office or in the house on the corner than there are living under bridges and in doorways. Once a person needs a mind-altering drug to live and survive, he is addicted.

After spending many hours talking with fellow addicts and reading and studying, I realize that everyone who suffers addiction seems to share a common underlying condition. I'll call that condition shame. In his book *Healing the Shame That Binds You,* John Bradshaw presents an exhaustive review of the causes of addiction. I will leave it to the professionals to define their terms and give a complete explanation of their experiences. I can only talk about what I see in most of us who are addicted and how the seemingly common condition of shame impacts all of us.

Mr. Bradshaw's work confirms my belief that addiction is a reaction to something that we perceive has happened or is happening—something that makes us feel "less than." For some reason or set of reasons, we were (or felt we were) unwanted. This thread of common shame is woven throughout the histories of all addicts and is shown in the life story of the founder of Alcoholics Anonymous (AA): Bill W. The book, *Not God*, by Ernest Kurtz tells us that Bill was born in Vermont and had a younger sister named Dorothy. When Bill was a young boy, his father abandoned the family. Sometime after the disappearance of his father, Bill's mother decided that she, too, wanted a new life. She also abandoned Bill and his sister. She left the children with her parents and moved to Boston to pursue a new career. As a young man, and as an old man, Bill felt he was responsible for his parents' actions. He carried that burden of shame, although unfounded, for the rest of his life. He always thought that it was his fault that his parents separated and he felt abandoned.

The sense of shame Bill felt is felt in different ways by most, if not all, alcoholics and addicts. Time after time, I have asked my fellows in the AA program if they have or have had a story similar to Bill's. Their answer has always been "yes." Most of us have had some event or series of events happen to us—usually at an early age—that caused us to believe we were inferior to other people. We had the sense we were, in one way or another, abandoned, unwanted, or were a genuine disappointment to our parents or primary caregivers. We were "less than," we were shamed.

A good example of this sense of "less than" can be illustrated by the case of an abandoned child sent to a foster home. In that new home, the child looks for the love and attention she craves.

Then for some reason, totally out of the child's control, she is moved to another foster home. Now her defenses are up, and her ability to have a healthy relationship with any new family, or in fact anyone, has been diminished if not destroyed. The child feels unwanted and unloved. She blames herself for being rejected, not only by her biological family, but by everyone else who is supposed to care for her.

This feeling of shame doesn't go away. This is not the same as the shame one demonstrates for getting caught with his hand in the cookie jar. The latter is normal feeling of guilt for something a person did wrong. The shame an addict feels is assumed or passed on from the primary caretaker or parent. The shame is experienced even though the child did nothing to deserve it; it is learned, and it is unfounded. This shame was not caused by any action of the child and is out of the child's control: but it is real. It is so real that it is likely to stay with the child throughout her life and may become a root of later addiction. It may become the overriding influence on her entire emotional life.

When we are damaged as children, the hurt is so strong that we, over time, develop mechanisms to protect ourselves. When we are hurt as defenseless children by circumstances that are out of our control, we will make countless efforts to be in control of our own lives and to avoid being hurt again. Defenses grow and are expressed by all sorts of common behaviors: lying, stealing, cheating, anger, resentment, arrogance and self-centeredness. We do all we can to protect ourselves from more hurt by building protective walls around ourselves. We believe that if we weren't good enough for our primary caretakers, we aren't good enough for anyone else either. Most of us withdraw from those around us and isolate ourselves. We don't want anyone to see inside us because we feel ashamed.

Others who are damaged as children hide by becoming the life of the party. They can always be counted on to go out, be loud, tell the jokes, and do something outrageous. The wall is still there; it is a wall of fake happiness that is just as tall and just as thick as any other. They allow no one to see the hurt and loneliness they really feel. The need to be lubricated before attending a social event or party is not necessarily a sign of alcoholism, but when the drinking reaches the point where the person is sneaking drinks on the sly and has to have the alcohol at all times, then there is a problem. Alcoholism can begin at a very early age when youngsters feel they fit in better when they have had a few drinks. I have met children in their early teens who have already experienced alcoholic blackouts because they have taken the use of alcohol past being a social stimulant and into the zone where they have to have it just to get through the day.

The shame or feeling "less than" does not always occur as a result of maltreatment by others in our early years. It can be caused by divorce, an untimely death, or a physical trait that we perceive to be wrong or different from everyone else such as being too short, too heavy, or the wrong color. We might have grown up ashamed of our family's socioeconomic status. Additionally, alcoholism can be hereditary, whether because of shared DNA or shared environment. For the alcoholic, the voices of shame are constantly buzzing in our heads telling us over and over that we are not good enough and can't let anyone find out that's how we really feel about ourselves.

When we took that first drink, or used our first drug, we finally found something to quiet the voices. We found a moment of peace, and we felt good about ourselves. However, we soon found that the bottle, the needle, and the pill are jealous lovers. Little by little, they start to consume more and more of us. We become so intent on escaping who we think we are that we become slaves to the escape. We are stuck inside ourselves with our only company being the self that we hate. So we drink or drug to dull the pain, which leads us to hate ourselves even more. The spiral of self-hatred and self-medication continues, and the shame grows and grows until we can't see anything else. We make sure that every bad thing that has ever been said about us becomes true. Jack Daniels numbed my shame for many years.

4

If self-shame is the basis of our problems, then it might stand to reason that all the potential alcoholic needs is a few classes on self-esteem. If we only felt good about ourselves, we wouldn't need to get drunk or use drugs. I believe, however, that we could attend all the classes and read all the self-help books out there and the outcome would be the same—alcoholism. Why? Because when we are in the depths of shame, it is impossible for us to truly hear anything anyone tells us that is positive. Our belief in our lack of worth closes our ears to anything but the voices in our heads constantly telling us that we are less than.

The emotional conflict that is set up as a result of carried shame is the basis for our anger, resentment, and fear, which in turn causes us to withdraw and isolate ourselves. The anger, resentment, and fear become the bricks we use to build walls that hide the truth of what we believe about ourselves. The higher we build the wall, the deeper we go into ourselves, the more we lose contact with reality. Unless we seek treatment, our ever-growing wall and resulting withdrawal can lead us to depression or insanity.

For me, the wall building began when I was a child. I was not abused or abandoned, but I was made to feel "less than." I was born in June 1941. I have a brother born in May 1940. My mother, having two babies in less than two years, was overwhelmed and sent me to live with her parents. The grandmother I was sent to live with told me numerous times when I was a young boy that "they," (whoever they were) prayed that I would be born a girl and when they found out I was a boy, they cried. Like the children removed from their biological parents at birth, I could sense as an infant that I was not what my parents wanted. There were many things my mother let me know that she did not like about me. She didn't like that I was a boy and that I came so soon after my brother. She even told me many times that she hated my name!

My mother also told me a story about how I had a nanny named Bertie. Although I don't remember Bertie, my mother often brought up to me that when I was scared by passing trains

I would run to Bertie and not to my mother. So, although my mother made it clear that she did not really want me around, she was insulted that I would run to another for comfort.

I can clearly remember when I was three or four years of age, walking with my brother in New York's Central Park. My brother was wearing a shirt that had his name printed on it. I also had on a shirt, but mine did not have my name on it. It merely said "Brother." To this day, I can remember adults laughing at that.

For years, the memory of their laughter brought with it an immediate recall of the feeling of wanting to rip their faces off for making fun of me. I don't remember who it was who laughed, and I'm sure the incident meant nothing to them and was forgotten immediately. But for forty years, that laughter stuck in my craw. The pattern of being "less than"—not as smart as, not as good as—went on for years. Inside, I was seething and my rebellion was growing. I suffered deeply from second-child syndrome and used it like a club. After reading John Bradshaw's work, I believe that every family has some level of dysfunction: some families more than others. My family wasn't off-the-charts dysfunctional, but significant damage was done to most, if not all my siblings. Unwittingly, this history set the foundation for my wall building.

As we build our walls of defense, the only one inside the walls is us. Our primary goal is to protect ourselves and as a result, everything becomes about us. What we see as self-protection, others see as selfishness. Until we can let go of thinking that everything is about us and our needs, we can't get better. We need to take the steps to the real world before we can recover.

One of my best AA buddies was a Catholic priest, Father Tom. He did unbelievable good for hundreds, if not thousands of AA members. He coined many pithy statements, and one of the best was "Give up all hope for a better past." Once the addict can grasp that concept, he or she will be ready to accept what AA has to offer.

Earlier, I said that I never knew unconditional love until there were grandchildren in my life. My wife put up with my controlling, angry nature. She is a saint. But when these beautiful, little creatures came along, I felt instant, pure, unconditional love. I acted not as the self-centered S.O.B. I had always been, because these children were instantly more important than anything or anyone, including me. One of the youngest grandchildren, a three-year-old boy, recently reminded me of who I was. The first time he went trick or treating on Halloween, he stood at the door as a woman put candy into his bag and the bags of two of his buddies. In the excitement of the moment, he did not see the candy being put into his bag. He saw only the other two boys receiving their treats. He looked up at the woman and said, "Hey! What about me?" At three years old, he was acting as I did at twenty-three, thirty-three, and forty-three years old.

God Is at the Meeting

I have a saying that my friends in Alcoholics Anonymous are probably tired of hearing: God hangs out at the meetings. He hangs out at other places too, but we alcoholics find Him there at the meetings. The importance of meetings can't be overstated; that is where one first learns about AA. Meetings are where the program comes alive. Meetings are where an addict realizes— perhaps for the first time—that he or she is not alone. Meetings are the lifeline you can grasp and hold onto as you walk into a life of recovery.

If you are just deciding to look into AA, you might wonder how to find out where the meetings are and when they are held. When I was looking for my first meeting, a friend produced a list of meeting places and times for the meetings in my city. I was amazed at the number of meetings and thought, *My God, are there that many alcoholics?*

It is easy to find meetings if you want to. Phone directories, including electronic ones, keep listings of Alcoholics Anonymous, with the address and phone number of the local central office. Don't get misled by the numbers for treatment centers. Perhaps you should consider them later, but for now look for AA or the AA hotline. In smaller towns, the local doctor or sheriff may be able to help you find the meeting places. Once you find the meeting place and time, muster the courage to go. No one there will care who you are or where you come from. You don't have to say a word. Just go to the meeting and listen. Your mind will be so confused that you most likely will not remember what you hear. That is just fine. Going is the important thing. Going back is more important.

If you are like most of us, you will pick a meeting away from your home with the expectation that no one will know you. That is okay. You will probably drive your spouse's car, wear your oldest clothes, and try not to make eye contact with anyone, and that is okay, too. You will probably park in the back of the lot, or you may even park a couple of blocks away. Isn't it funny? You never cared if your neighbors saw your car at the local bar, but you will care a lot if they see your car in front of an AA meeting place.

You will find that there are open meetings that may include men, women, businessmen, college students and all other walks of life. There are also meetings geared to specific groups. There are meetings specifically for women and groups only for men; there are groups for gays; groups for motorcycle riders and groups for Native Americans. There are meetings where the cigarette smoke is so heavy you may have trouble seeing the person sitting across from you and there are those where no smoking is allowed. Find the group where you are most comfortable and feel that you will find the support you need.

At your first meeting, or in fact at any meeting, you are not required to say anything until you are ready to do so. If you are called on and don't want to speak, just say, "I'll pass." No one will think less of you, no one will judge why you aren't ready to speak to the group. The meetings probably won't help much until you stop passing, but you will know when it is time to actively participate. No one is counting heads, unless you are sent to the meeting by a court. In that case, the court will count the meetings you attend, but no one at the meeting will keep track of your attendance. No one at the meeting will care why you are there. They will assume you want to stop drinking or using and treat you accordingly. That is what everyone else is there for, and you will be welcome to join in when you are ready.

One question most newcomers have is, "what is a sponsor and how do I find one?" My answer is, in my case, after a few months of attending meetings an old-timer named Henry asked me if I had a sponsor. I told him I did not and he asked, "why not?" I told him I did not know who to ask. He advised me, bluntly, "find someone." I said, "Okay, will you be my sponsor?" His answer was, "yes." At the time I didn't know how valuable he would become to me. I can't enumerate the ways he helped me. It was a new experience to have a man on my side. Up until that time, I saw all other men as rivals. This was the beginning of a major change in my life. He never judged me, never told me what to do (however, his wife did). He showed me how to live and how the program had worked for him. At the time he was sober 20 years. I encourage you not to be as dense as I was; find a sponsor sooner rather than later.

So what is a sponsor? A sponsor is a person you select to guide you through the Steps. If he or she becomes a friend, so be it, but that is not their primary purpose. You choose your sponsor and it should be someone with whom you will feel comfortable and who you believe you can trust. This person will learn what you believe to be your deepest, darkest secrets so should be someone you believe has your best interests at heart. I personally believe this person should have several years in the program and have built a strong foundation. Try to find a person who has common life experiences.

Understand that your sponsor may not be your sponsor for life. You may find that the person you relate to in the beginning is not the one to take you through all the Steps. In AA it is perfectly acceptable to "fire" your sponsor and your sponsor will not be offended. In some cases, your sponsor may be the one to suggest that you need to find someone else. This is okay too.

It is not imperative that you find a sponsor at your first meeting, your fifth meeting or even your tenth meeting, but it is imperative that you find a sponsor before you begin taking the Steps that will lead you to sobriety, so the sooner, the better. If you're not immediately drawn to someone in your regular meeting, go to other meetings until you find someone to whom you can relate. This is something it would be wise to pray over and ask God for direction.

There is no timetable in AA. I probably went to twenty or so meetings before I admitted, "I am an alcoholic." Prior to that admission, if I introduced myself, I would just say my name and not attach the horrid title of alcoholic. Today, some twenty-five years later, I know it was the best admission I ever made. In fact, today I am grateful for being an alcoholic because recovery from that condition has changed me and my life. I probably would never have changed, would never have stayed as part of my family, and would never have come to love my God as I do today. Truthfully, I would probably be dead, in prison, or in a mental institution.

In AA, I found a community I could understand and one that could understand me. I believe that, as alcoholics, we need to live in a community in order to develop a spiritual life. Others have families, places of worship, clubs, military groups, and sports teams, but it is a fact for me and most other addicts that we cannot get out of ourselves and find sobriety without a community to encourage, support, and correct us. The acceptance we are forever seeking happens in the ranks of AA. In AA, we can be ourselves, and we accept each other. Again, when you walk into an AA meeting, no one will care where you came from or who you are. They only need to know you are an alcoholic who is seeking help in AA. This acceptance begins to fill the void of acceptance we experienced as young people.

Sameness was something I previously rejected. I didn't get enough attention as a youngster, so I was determined to make up for lost time. This intense need to be different, to stand out from the crowd, came home to me one night while I was attending a meeting in Omaha. The room in which we were meeting had a large poster of lady bugs—hundreds of lady bugs, all of them looking exactly the same. The thought hit me, "If I were a ladybug, I would need my shell to be lit up in neon so people would look at me, look at me, look at me."

While we are in many ways similar to our brother or sister alcoholics, we are also each unique works of God's art. For me, this new community, this new family, gives me what I didn't receive as a child. It is welcoming, kind, nonjudgmental, and unconditionally loving. I became part of it, and it allowed me to grow into being me. The *Big Book* speaks of being reborn; we get a start at living in a real world.

If a practicing addict or alcoholic begins to attend meetings, he has a chance to feel, if not see, the power of God. Those of us who stay around for any length of time not only feel it, we also see it and become proof of it. We see God do for people what they cannot do for themselves. We see the sorriest cases recover. We see people brought from the threshold of death to life. We see real miracles happen every day. We find the freedom to consider our own recovery a true miracle.

The satisfaction and good feeling of seeing others recover is wonderful. This high is better and longer lasting than anything booze bought us. In AA, we see young men or women who have been causing their families untold heartache become nice people. We hear the senior citizen who found the doors of AA in his or her sixties or later say, "These are the best days of my life." We see men and women come out of jail or prison and become upstanding and reliable members of society who, maybe for the first time, can care for their families.

The changes are so great that they are unbelievable. God does hang out at meetings. A middle-aged man I know who regularly attends meetings told the group that he spent two terms in prison. One term was for two years and the second for six. When he got out the second time, he went back to his old ways and was arrested as a result of his drinking. At this arrest he faced two choices: prison again or sobriety. Chances are he thought of sobriety as a sentence, but he chose to get sober rather than go back to prison. Today, after many years in the free world and in AA, he attributes his sobriety and spiritual life to AA. He tells us he had a spiritual awakening, and if you knew him, you would believe him. He is a new man and a very productive member of AA.

A spiritual awakening is different from a spiritual experience. A spiritual experience comes usually like a clap of thunder. We become aware that God is sending us a message. In his book, *Bill Wilson and Alcoholics Anonymous*, author Ervin Shaw reported that Bill W. described his spiritual experience as "seeing a great white light." For most of us, spiritual awakening usually occurs as a result of learning and living the Steps. It is an ever-growing awareness of our dependence on God and rejection of selfishness.

The former inmate mentioned above told us something he learned many years ago. He told us that when considering giving AA a try, one should consider AA to be a slow process of change and surrender. When he entered AA, he said he heard two voices talking to him all the time. It was like having a dog on each shoulder: a good dog, small like a Chihuahua, on one shoulder and an evil dog like a Rottweiler on the other. The little dog yapped and yapped while the big dog barked hard and loud. As time went on, the little dog's voice got louder and the big dog's voice softer. As the years went by, the good voice got louder while the evil voice got softer and softer. It is clear that if he continues his life in AA, there is little to no chance he will wind up in prison again. A life has been saved and transformed, as have all the lives in which he is involved. This same transformation is available to you.

Step One

We Admitted We Were Powerless Over Alcohol – That Our Lives Had Become Unmanageable

When I first heard this Step, it meant nothing to me. What is this powerless stuff? I was forty-four years old. I had a great job, a big house, a wife and kids, and it all looked great. Okay, I drank every single day and my best friend was Jack Daniels, but I was not powerless. I was always stressed out, anxious, and angry. People who knew me were afraid of me, including my wife and children. That was my normal state. In my mind, drinking was necessary; it was the only thing that calmed me down. It was my one and only way of escaping the imagined pressures of life. Over the years, I was employed by some of the best brokerage firms in the country. I was their regional and then national sales manager. I flew all over the country speaking at sales meetings and investor seminars. I was that so-called expert—the guy from out of town with the briefcase. The friendly skies were my second home. I have traveled more than a million miles sitting in airline seats.

My primary task was giving seminars and sales meetings for brokers and their clients. I got pretty good at it and was able to make a very good living. I was always under pressure to get from one meeting to another as I traveled around the country. There were many times when my sales territory was the entire fifty states. Over the years, I visited them all. When I was giving a sales presentation or seminar, I was the center of attention, and

I was a happy boy because I was in the limelight. I don't think I was chasing the good life as much as I was running away from something. I didn't know what I was running from or, in fact, that I was running. But I now know that I used my pursuit of my career as a cover for running from myself. I ran from the constant awareness that I wasn't good enough.

I didn't think my life was unmanageable. In fact, I very carefully managed to plan my day around drinking. My friend Jack and I managed to spend hundreds of nights together in hotel rooms with very little trouble. I managed to keep up a good front . . . most of the time. There may be a good number of airline attendants and hotel clerks who would not agree with that statement.

I was gone from home most of the time for years. My wife did the job of raising our three sons, and that was a good thing for them. On numerous occasions, my drinking caught up with me, but I always got away with it. No one except my wife ever confronted me about my drinking and stupid behavior. Recently one of my sons moved to a town where we lived many years ago. Usually I have had good connections in the places where I lived, but on this occasion, I had to tell my son, "Can't help you there. That is where I did most of my drinking damage. I doubt that anyone would be glad to welcome me or any of my family back."

There was a time when I worked for a small firm in Denver. One day, during lunch, I went drinking with some of my fellow employees. When we came back, something happened. I truthfully don't even remember the trigger, but sales were slow and I was getting pressure to get better results. I remember getting very angry at my boss. It was his fault, don't you know, that I was not succeeding. Since he wasn't there, I decided to take my hostility out on his office. I made numerous attempts to throw his desk out the third-floor window. The damn window wouldn't break, so I tried to throw the desk over and over again. I wrecked the place and made a hell of a mess of his office. The next day the office manager, who was a good guy, explained to my fellow employees that I "worked hard and needed to play hard." The case was closed, and I never heard about it again. Yes, my life was totally under control and manageable.

During all my drinking days, I was very active in my church. I gave away a fair amount of money and devoted some time to church projects. I prayed for sobriety—at least I thought I did—but for some reason never had the sense that God would work directly in my life. This is a pretty weird self-analysis because if you had asked me at the time if God would work in your life, the answer would be a resounding, "Yes! Yours, but not mine." That must say something about who I was or who I thought I was. I saw myself as someone gifted who didn't need God's help or, conversely, as that unwanted kid who wasn't worthy of God's help. I generously allowed God to save His time for the poor and downtrodden. He gave me enough to make it on my own. What a joke. The poor and downtrodden were, and are, a lot smarter than me. They had their God working in their lives. I was on my own. That was the most honest statement I could make at that time.

Years after the incident in Denver, on one of my business trips I got very sick with chest pains, the whole nine yards. I wound up in the hospital for four days and had the horrible verdict, or more rightly diagnosis, of alcoholism. The doctor, whom I still call my guardian angel, told me to stop drinking and if I couldn't, to come back and tell him. That is a pretty dumb thing to say to an alcoholic: "Come back and tell me if you can't stop drinking." We never listen. We don't think we need help. The last thing I wanted to be told was that I needed to slow down my drinking. My thought, as yours probably has been, was, "I can do it on my own." In fact, I quit drinking every single night when I would either fall asleep or pass out. I saw that doctor recently and thanked him for his diagnosis. I told him how appreciative I am. He is a great man, and on that day twenty-five years ago, he was God's mouthpiece.

Dr. Mike was actually the fourth doctor to tell me to stop drinking, but the only one to offer a hand if I wanted it. In the

AA lingo, we talk about moments of clarity. Well, I must have had one, because three or four weeks later I went back to see Dr. Mike and admitted, "I can't stop." He introduced me to one of his associates, a doctor and longtime member of AA. Dr. Cal introduced me to AA, of which I had known nothing. He gave me a list of AA meetings near my home and told me to try the meetings.

That first meeting was a thing to behold. It was held in a church basement. Big executive that I was, I drove my pick-up truck to the meeting place. God forbid anyone would see my car there. Over the years I have laughed at people like me who have no problem if all their friends see them drunk in the bar but use all their creativity to try to hide their attendance at AA. We can't let anyone know that we are "one of them."

At that first meeting, I wasn't too anxious. I was more curious and somewhat embarrassed. When I went in, no one asked me who I was. They just welcomed me as one of the group. None of them knew I thought of myself as a big-shot, that I was mister executive who had a big house and three cars and was the main speaker at business meetings all around the country. Somehow they just didn't care. Again, thank You, God. Mostly women and youngsters attended the meeting. They smoked too much and drank too much coffee. I remember nothing of what was said. All I knew was that I had been digging and digging to get out of the hole I was in and had dug long enough to finally reach rock bottom. I couldn't take life any longer as I was living it. If I didn't stop digging, I was convinced I would go nuts or go to jail or I would have to kill myself.

The next day I did what Dr. Cal told me to do—I went to another meeting. I must admit that I really didn't believe the folks there who said they had sixty days of sobriety; much less the people who claimed to have five years. That is like a frickin' eternity for an alcoholic. I didn't believe them because I thought they were like me: not very good at telling the truth. "Soon," I thought, "they will tell me the secret." Of course, I wanted the secret to be that it was okay to drink if I only . . . Like most who have tried to quit before, I didn't think it was possible to totally quit. I just needed the secret for cutting down on my drinking. I truly believed that if I hung around long enough and behaved, I would eventually be told the truth. I believed that newcomers were probably told one thing but that people who had "made it" were secretly told where the real meetings were—the ones where some drinking was okay. I absolutely did not believe it was possible to live without drinking.

Another life-changer occurred at that second meeting, a fellow handed me a copy of the *Big Book* and told me to read it. At that point I had no idea what the *Big Book* was, nor did I have a clue where to find one, so I was grateful for his gift. I took the book home and read it that day. The first time through the book, it didn't make any sense to me. The second and third times weren't much better, but I had seen the program work for others and was determined to understand what they were talking about. A couple of months after receiving the book, I had to fly to Hawaii. The *Big Book* was my companion on that trip, taking the place of my old traveling companion, Jack Daniels. By then the words of the book had begun to make sense and provide the comfort that I needed.

A few years later, again on a flight, I was again reading through the *Big Book*. The gentleman sitting next to me kept reading over my shoulder. He was, and is, a nationally-known television personality. When I asked him about his interest in the book, he offered to me that he was addicted to Valium, but was afraid to go to meetings because he was so well known. I offered him my copy of the book, which he graciously accepted. I hope he still has it or has passed it on to someone else in need.

For most of my life, I never did what I was told, but when Dr. Cal advised me to go to ninety meetings in ninety days, I followed his advice. I realized, and you hear this a lot, I was sick and tired of being sick and tired and was finally ready to reach out for help. My first meeting was on November 25, 1985, and I have not had a drink since. I finally stopped fighting. I knew I was drinking too much, and I had proof it was killing me and hurting my family. There was no more denying who I was and what I had become— an alcoholic. This admission—and reaching out for help—was my first act of humility. The program emphasizes the importance of humility, but the word humility is one that might scare you as much as the word spirituality. According to *Webster's New World Dictionary*, humility simply means earthy, on the ground, not proud or haughty, not arrogant or assertive. It doesn't mean you are required to be submissive, passive, or self-deprecating; it just means that you have your feet on the ground and that you can give up the effort to be the center of the universe. It means being willing to be teachable.

I have to say that in not one of those first ninety meetings was the secret to drinking less ever revealed. AA wastes no time in attempting to teach us how not to drink. Not even one lesson. It goes right to the problem, which is not the drink but the drinker. For most of us, alcohol is not the problem to be solved; rather, it is a temporary solution to the living problem. Sometime during those ninety days I realized that I needed help and I couldn't find the way out on my own. I came to believe that AA might be the help I needed and was truly happy and full of hope for the first time in many years.

The importance of meetings cannot be overstated; that is where one first learns about AA and where the program comes alive. It is where you will realize you are not alone. For most of us, it is the first time in our entire lives when we don't feel alone.

I believe God hangs out in meetings. He does. Of course, He hangs out at other places as well, but for the alcoholic, the meeting is where God is revealed. The miracles that begin at these meetings are beyond belief. They are miracles in every sense of the word. God does do for us what we cannot do for ourselves.

Maurice C.

Step One—Ask Yourself:

1. Do I really want help?
2. Will I accept that help?
3. Do I have any doubts that I am an alcoholic?
4. Have I reached rock bottom?
5. My first meeting was _____ (date)
6. My second meeting was _____ (date)
7. My third meeting was _____ (date)

Step Two

Came to Believe That a Power Greater than Ourselves Could Restore Us to Sanity

Many newcomers question the use of the word sanity in this Step because they believe they are perfectly sane; they are merely drunks. However, alcoholics and addicts, as a result of their wall building and self-protection, live in a make-believe world. If you are drinking daily, drinking is destroying your family, drinking is threatening your job, and alcohol is running your life, you are living in an insane world. Sanity is nothing other than living in the real world. The real world is this: life won't get better simply by wishing for it, no matter how hard you wish.

A friend told me recently that his drinking is getting out of hand, and he wanted to know if having blackouts was a bad sign. I told him that it was obvious that if he was drinking to the point of blacking out, he needed to seek help. His response was, "I don't want to do that now." I asked him to please be sure to not drive when he was in a state of blackout, and he assured me he wouldn't. He failed to acknowledge that, while in a state of blackout, we have no control over what we do. He might drive and not even know or remember that he did. I have two good friends who were both incarcerated for twenty-plus years for killing another person while they were in a blackout. They didn't know who they killed or why. That is insanity.

My own insanity persisted for years. I tried all the usual things to stop or slow down my drinking. Nothing worked. My wife, doctors, psychologists, and priests could not tell me how to stop. They all told me I needed to stop, but none offered any solution until I met Dr. Mike. During my ninety meetings in ninety days, I finally admitted to myself that I could not quit drinking on my own, but I never thought my God would be willing to remove the addiction for me. That was not His job; He was busy taking care of the sick. I was too cool to be needy. Either I would figure out the answer or there just would not be an answer. I no longer denied that I was an alcoholic, but I was still trying to deny my own inability to cure myself.

The second Step of AA says that we came to believe a Power greater than ourselves could restore us to sanity. A simple understanding of this Step came to me rather quickly. I didn't get hung up on who or what this Power is or was. I was told it was simply a power greater than me, and I was not the power. At that time, that was all I needed to know. My power had run out. I was beat when I got to the doors of AA. My wife told me that I had reached the point of desperation. I had reached rock bottom.

For me the bottom was more an emotional and psychological bottom than a financial bottom. I just couldn't take life the way I was living it any more. Jack Daniels, who had been my intimate friend for years, stopped working for me. In the early years, drinking gave me a lift. As time went by, it became a crutch to get me through the stress of everyday living. I thought stress came from the outside—my schedule, my responsibilities, and so on. I didn't realize that my stress came not from my life but from my reactions to my life.

I couldn't cope with life and needed a crutch, and that crutch was alcohol. Then drinking became more than a crutch; it became a necessity. Finally, I was at the point when I was tired of fighting life, I had been digging my ditch so long and so hard I was exhausted. I couldn't lift my shovel even one more time. Toward the end, there were times when just a few drinks were too many and other times when a fifth wasn't enough. The worst part was that it stopped working. I didn't get a lift or even get high. The stuff stopped solving all my problems, and I reached what we call the "jumping-off place." I had to stop it or it would stop me.

I soon found that going to "those" meetings was a relief and a blessing. I found a place of peace. I didn't know what was going on, but I knew it was good. Dozens of guys and gals who I came to love would start off saying, "I'm Dick, and I'm an alcoholic," or "I'm Mary, and I'm an alcoholic," and they really were not drinking. I watched these folks. AA worked for them, and they seemed truly content and happy. I thought, "Holy s—, it might work for me too!"

One statement you will hear at AA and from AA members is, "Take it one day at a time." When I first heard the concept of one day at a time I thought it was one of the dumbest things I ever heard. I was in a business that was dynamic. We planned months and years in advance. I, perhaps like you, was always trained to plan ahead for everything. I planned my career moves, planned to save for my kids' college, planned how to spend my leisure time, and planned my retirement years in advance. Living for only the day at hand was foreign to me. What I learned from AA was not to live in the future, any more than I should live in the past.

When I first started AA, if I had thought that I was going to have to stay sober for the next 30 years, I would have panicked. AA taught me to focus on staying sober today. Tomorrow I will focus on being sober tomorrow. I can honestly say that one day at a time becomes easier and easier until the focus changes from staying sober to actually living life. If you are one of us, those statements make sense. If you are not, they don't.

Another thing you might hear said at AA is, "I am not much, but I'm all I think about." We are egomaniacs with an inferiority complex. Virtually everyone I have met in the program suffers from one common disease—selfishness. We see life only through the prism of ourselves. No matter what is going on, we want to know first and foremost, "How does this affect me? What will I stand to gain or lose?" We become so self-focused that we can't get out of our own way.

Because we are egomaniacs, we believe the whole world revolves around us. Deep on the inside we feel we are inferior, so we can't believe there are others who see us as valuable. The ego side tells us we can solve our own problems, while the inferiority tells us that we will never be good enough. We somehow think everyone else is exactly as they seem on the outside. If they are smiling on the outside, we believe they are happy on the inside. If they are well dressed and well groomed, we assume they have their lives together. Because we live with the idea that we are "less than," we believe we are the only ones who are hiding what's on the inside. Don't fall into the temptation of comparing your insides with others' outsides. You will learn that all addicts, and indeed probably most people, are hiding things from outside view.

What you will find in AA is that you are accepted no matter who you are, who you think you are, or what you have done. There is no judgment, only acceptance. If you are attending meetings where there is judgment or non-acceptance, find another. AA does not accept or condone our misdeeds or breaking the law of either God or man, but it does look through them. It sees a person, good inside, who has done some really stupid things. AA will reach out a hand to lead you to do good things. The acceptance opens the door for each of us to begin to believe there is good inside. When I got to AA, I was worn out and tired of fighting life, and as I said before, my wife told me I had reached the point of desperation.

As I attended the meetings and observed the men and women there, all of whom claimed they were alcoholics, I saw people who were happy, content, and even joyful. Joy was long gone from my life. I clearly remember becoming angry and agitated at meetings when the regular meeting goers would laugh and be frivolous at the meetings. I thought they failed to see how serious my problem was and that they weren't taking me seriously enough. Again, it was all about me. While they did treat the problem of alcoholism seriously, they didn't take me nearly as seriously as I took myself.

In short, simply by observing the people at the meetings living happily and hopefully, I began to believe that the power that relieved their burden could relieve mine. For me, life had become a chore. It was hard and dreary work. My life had no fun in it. My perceived problems had become so all-consuming that there was just no time for fun.

Then something happened to me that might seem insignificant to many but was an "aha" moment for me. After some weeks of attending meetings, I was on my way to a Saturday-morning breakfast meeting and I heard birds singing. I, who used to love nature and spent as much time as possible outdoors, hadn't heard birds in years. That Power that was helping my fellow alcoholics was helping me. I came to believe that, with that Power, I could joyfully live in the real world again. I honestly believe that a Power greater than myself can, and did, restore me to sanity. That Power is available to anyone who has an open mind and heart.

If you are at the place where there is no joy in your life, where life is such a burden that you're not sure you can face another day, seek help. If alcohol has gone from friend to crutch to no longer working at all, find a group of people who have been where you are. If your own power has failed you and you recognize that you cannot heal yourself, seek a Higher Power who can, and will heal you.

The act of coming to believe in a Power outside ourselves is an act of humility. Alcoholics, as a group, are not humble. Even if it happens slowly, we have to learn what humility is. It may take a lifetime to learn how to be humble. It goes against our nature to put other people and their needs first. We have spent most of our lives trying to run the show of life, always trying to arrange things and people to serve ourselves. When we put our selfishness aside, little by little we begin to live with humility. God seems to show up at moments of humility. In fact, we come to expect His presence. Humility opens the window to God's power. The more I open the window, the better my chances of getting in the path of His grace.

I think of humility as a stream of grace coming from God. Sometimes it's a trickle, sometimes a river, and sometimes that grace of humility is an ocean. The more time I spend in that stream, the better off I am. Making the admission that we are powerless, asking for help, showing up at meetings, living the Steps, and praying for the knowledge of His will and the power to carry that out are all acts of humility. Moments of humility, however brief, are necessary to receive the gift of sobriety.

Step Two—Ask Yourself:

1. When did you take the second Step?
2. Was it something gradual?
3. Why did you take it?
4. What regular meetings were you attending when you realized you had taken the Step?
5. Who were the people who helped you come to believe?
6. Have you found a sponsor yet, even a temporary one?
7. Have you settled on a home group? This is the group you will meet with every week, no matter what.
8. Does the word humility scare you?

Step Three

Made a Decision to Turn Our Will and Our Lives Over to the Care of God as We Understood Him

At most AA meetings, we will read the first few paragraphs of chapter five in the *Big Book—How it Works*. The reading usually ends with the beautiful prayer in what we call the ABCs:

a) That we were alcoholic and probably could not manage our own lives
b) That probably no human power could have relieved our alcoholism
c) That God could and would if He were sought

When we can agree with the language of the ABCs, we are ready to take the third Step. We have surrendered to the fact that we are alcoholic and are unable to do anything about that fact. We understand and believe no human power can relieve our addiction, especially our own human power. The next logical step, then, is to find the Power who can relieve our addiction to alcohol.

This is really simple, but leave it to alcoholics to complicate it. We made a decision to turn our will and our lives over to the care of God as we understand Him. We simply made a decision. Take as an example: I can make a decision to go to the next Super Bowl game. I may not know who is playing, where it is being held, or the exact date; I just make the decision to go. That is all the Step calls for—a decision. I decide to turn my will and life over to the care of God as I understand Him. I don't need to know what my will and life are and sure don't need to define God.

When you hear people discuss this Step at meetings, you will hear all kinds of concerns. Some will ask, "What is this God stuff? Just who is the God you are talking about?" Fortunately, the authors of the *Big Book* solve the problem of God by telling us He is the God you understand. You are not asked to convert or change beliefs, as it is the God of your understanding.

In the first Step, we basically admitted that we have a problem we can't handle on our own. In the second Step, we agreed there is a Power greater than us who can help us with that problem. The logical thing now is just to ask that Power for help. When taking this Step, my sponsor encouraged me to formalize my decision. This decision was for the long term. The rest of the Steps would show me how to implement this Step. Once I formally decided in front of my sponsor, the Step was in place unless or until I formally reject it.

For me, the time for the formal decision came when I finally realized and admitted that I had to depend on God. I needed His help, just as the sick and needy do. I was helpless to solve my drinking problem. This moment for me was a life changer. For the first time I can remember, I asked for help. I was previously too proud to ask for help for anything because I feared asking would show weakness. Admission of weakness was almost impossible for me because I was always trying to hide who I was. Asking for help was my first attempt at breaking down the walls of self-protection I had so carefully built. Today, twenty-five years later, asking for help is still not natural for me. Harder yet is accepting help. How stupid must I be to not welcome help from anyone, especially my Higher Power. If we want to be rid of a life of addiction, we each have to ask for help, accept the help, and put ourselves in the hands of the One who cares for us most.

Let's talk about God for a minute. A lot of folks get hung up on this subject. My advice is to just be patient. Some folks become afraid they are going to have to believe in a God manufactured by AA. Maybe they have a problem with any notion of any God. The AA literature addresses those questions brilliantly. Don't get hung up on God. He knows who He is, even if you don't. If this is a problem for you, see if you can't come to an agreement simply that you are not God. That is all you need to start. If you persist in the program, you will grow in your knowledge and awareness of God. As one of my old buddies said, "Just take it from me, there is a God, and it isn't you!" If you cannot believe in God, or you are very angry at God as you know him, at least believe that, in AA, there are people who have been where you are who will listen to you and lead you. The critical thing is that the Power is outside of you. Believe it or not, there is real Power outside of you—a tough lesson for alcoholics to learn.

I urge you to not think of your Higher Power as being so high and so distant that He doesn't care about you personally. As strange as the idea may seem, while you are attempting to draw closer to the Higher Power, He is drawing closer to you. He cares for you on a personal, daily, minute-by-minute basis. A few weeks into the program, and while doing my ninety in ninety, I had a startling experience that showed me how close God was. I had stopped into a church with the intention of saying a few prayers. The church was empty, and I sat down with the hope of settling my mind. After sitting for only two minutes, my maximum attention span, I got up and walked back to the car. I was full of frustration, confused and on edge. Newly off the booze, my brain was racing, and I just couldn't stay still very long. On the way to the car, I looked up at the sky and humbly begged, "God, please help me." To my surprise, I heard a voice—a loud voice—say, "I am." Today I still believe it was the voice of God. I am not nuts, and I don't usually hear voices, but I heard this one. Hearing His voice was a spiritual experience for me, a sign from God that I was on the right path.

If you are any kind of Bible reader, the words "I am" have a powerful meaning. Was my God talking to me? I think so, and I pray that you hear His voice in whatever way He speaks to you. Stick with the program and He will speak to you, sometimes loudly, sometimes softly. As long as we are willing to put our selfishness aside, He will show up. It seems that He always does.

I grew up in a religious family. All my school years were in parochial schools. I really didn't have any problem believing in God. In fact I had, and have, a great faith in God. While I believed in God, I didn't act as if I were one of His children. I was told as a child that I was unworthy, and I believed that. Maybe because of my hard heart, God was more a concept than a loving Father. Many of us have never, ever experienced true love from an earthly father or may have even had an earthly father who was cruel or abusive. Today I encourage all who struggle with the concept of God to imagine the most wonderful, loving, forgiving, nurturing being you can. Don't shortchange your understanding or concept of God. No matter how wonderful your concept may be, it is still too small to match reality. We witness proof of God's love and AA members come to expect miracles. If you attend meetings regularly, you will see miracles too.

This little story may not rank up there with a miracle, but it makes my point about a Higher Power working. My wife and I were busy at home in Council Bluffs, Iowa, and had been so for a number of weeks. On a Tuesday at noon, I told my wife I had to get out of the house and go play golf. There is a nearby golf course, so I grabbed my clubs, and off I went. When I got to the first tee, there were two twosomes waiting to tee off; two young men and an older couple. They were not going to join each other and were having a pleasant discussion as to who might go first. The young men encouraged the couple to play first and said they would be glad to play behind them.

I asked the four of them if I might join the couple. The young men had no complaint. If the couple did, it was too late, as I joined them on the first tee. We each hit our golf ball before we had a chance to introduce ourselves, and when we drove onto the fairway, I introduced myself to two lovely folks, Barry and his wife, Alice. They were on a road trip from Edmonton, Alberta, Canada, on their way to San Antonio, Texas. I told them I spend a fair amount of time in Texas, and Barry shot out that they were on their way to the AA worldwide convention. I said, "Good for you. I have almost twenty-five years in the fellowship." Barry said, "Good for you too. I have thirty and Alice thirty-two years."

Now I can't stretch that encounter into a real miracle, but I think it is more than happenstance. The fact that two Canadians out of Edmonton, Alberta, were in Council Bluffs, Iowa, and wanted to play golf that Tuesday at noon and met on the course a fellow AA is more than coincidence. Coincidences are God's way of staying anonymous. After golf, Barry and Alice joined me that evening in attending my home group meeting. Afterward I took Barry and Alice back to their campground. Barry said, "You know, I wasn't surprised we met up. I have come to expect that kind of thing to happen."

Besides learning about leaning on a Higher Power, Step Three has another lesson to teach us, and this one is uncomfortable. We learn in Step Three that we are selfish to the extreme. I didn't really understand this until I finished my first draft of my Fourth and Fifth Steps. I have yet to meet a newcomer who thought he or she was selfish. The truth is, most of us, when we get to the doors of AA, see ourselves as anything but selfish. We are the victims. Aren't we always taking care of people, places, and things? Aren't we always being put upon? Aren't we the folks who always have to work harder than the rest? The least understood? But that is it, folks—selfishness and self-centeredness. Today I know that every AA meeting I attend is attended by a bunch of selfish, self-centered people, and I am one of them. For right now it doesn't matter why we are so self-centered. It matters only that we believe it to be the truth. The root of my problems is *not* alcohol or drugs. The root of my problems is me.

According to Webster's New World Dictionary, selfishness is defined as caring unduly or supremely for oneself; regarding one's own comfort, advantage, etc., in disregard, or at the expense of that of others. This selfishness is the result of a life history of protecting the inner child described earlier. In an all-out effort to protect ourselves, we became so self-focused that we really didn't give a hoot about anyone else. Selfishness and self-protection became our default reaction in every situation. Our first thought was always, "How does this affect me?"

Some people may tell you that joining AA and doing the Steps is selfish because we are doing the program for ourselves. I don't want to get into semantics, but the program is anything but selfish. Sure, we benefit from the program and we are doing it for ourselves, but we are also doing what God wants. We are conforming our will to His, and we now know that that is the proper use of our will. The benefits of our sobriety flow not only to us but to everyone with whom we come into contact.

If you read the account of Adam and Eve in the first chapters of the book of Genesis in the Holy Bible, their sin is reported as an act of disobedience. But in the creation story, the Bible also says that they wanted to be like God. They ate the forbidden fruit with the expectation that, as Satan told them, they would be like God. Maybe Adam and Eve's action was not so much an act of disobedience as it was an act of pure selfishness. What and who they were was not enough; they wanted more. Being God's creation wasn't enough. They wanted to be equal to God. What an insult it is to God when we are not satisfied with who we are! Many of us have spent our entire lives trying to be someone else, trying on different personas to see if we can find the one that will allow us to fit in. Through seeking God, we learn that if we are good enough for Him, we ought to be good enough for ourselves. He loves us no matter how big and ugly our warts. Even if He does not love our actions, He loves us. We are His!

When we have accepted that we need a Higher Power, we have to come to grips with the fact that there is a new center in our lives. It may take us a lifetime to learn that we are not in charge of the world, politics, the weather, our spouses, our children, our bosses, our grandchildren, or our neighbors. This is God's world, not ours, and the truth is, we've always been in His care. We just didn't know it. When this awareness sinks in, it is a huge relief to know that we no longer have the job of running anything. The only thing we can run properly, and that only with God's help, is our own lives.

Once you can accept that you don't have to run the world, you no longer have to fight life. You can join the folks going with the flow of life instead of living with the exhaustion of constantly swimming upstream, always fighting everything and everybody. When we let God's love and grace into our hearts, the fight will be over, and life will not be so darned exhausting.

At most AA meetings you will hear the Serenity Prayer. We ask God for the serenity, not the power, to change the things in this world that we can change. The sooner we ask God for serenity, the sooner we conclude that the only thing we can change is ourselves.

Every time I think about this Step of recognizing a Higher Power and letting Him rule our lives, I think of the illustration Jesus used in the story of the prodigal son. This Bible story, found in the Book of Luke, Chapter 11, verses 11-32, is of a wealthy farmer and his two sons. The younger son, not wanting to wait until his father died to get his hands on the father's money, asked for his inheritance early so he could go out and make his own way. Well, it turns out his way was the way of a lot of fun and games. He blew the money on wine, women, and whatever pleasure he could buy. He made lots of friends, all eager to help him spend his inheritance. They were the same kind of friends we make while sitting on a barstool—the kind who stay around until the money runs out.

When his inheritance was exhausted and all his new friends had deserted him (sounds like an alcoholic), he lived like a pauper, jealous even of the pigs on his father's farm because at least the pigs were fed every day. In time, after he got sick and tired of being sick and tired, he reached rock bottom. He made the decision to return to his father and beg to be allowed to work, even to be counted as a slave so he could survive. When the father saw his son returning (it seems the father was always watching out for his son's return), the son was taken in and treated like a hero. The father threw a big feast and welcomed the young man, now wiser and worn, home and back to the family.

At this display of generosity of the father, the older brother, who had stayed home and worked faithfully, became quite upset with the father's generosity. He complained that no party was given for him, even though he had been the faithful son. The father tried to calm him down, explaining how happy he was that his younger son had come home and that the father was always there for the faithful son.

When I first thought about this parable, I thought it was about the money and inheritance. But it is not; it is about the love of a father for his son. The faithful son missed the point. His faithfulness was better served by the love of the father than the rewards of his physical work. The father's true gift to his sons was his love and affection, not their inheritance. The care our Father has for us is beyond any care we could have for ourselves. Like the father in the story, our Father is always lovingly on the watch for us, waiting for us to come home. We should never fear putting our lives in His hands.

Step Three—Ask Yourself:

1. When did you take the third Step?
2. Did you do it formally with a sponsor?
3. Are you attending Step and tradition meetings?
4. Can you look back now, reviewing the first three Steps, and believe what you have accomplished so far?
5. Has the desire for drink and/or drugs disappeared or been diminished?
6. Is your decision firm? If not, talk to your sponsor and go back to Step One.

Step Four

Made a Searching and Fearless Moral Inventory of Ourselves

All right, at this point we are willing to move forward. We have taken the Third Step and made the decision to turn our will and our lives over to the care of God. For me, I said the words admitting to Henry, my sponsor, that I had decided to turn my will and life over, but until I did the work of Steps Four and Five, I had no idea what my will and my life were. In this Step, you will search inside yourself without fear and write your moral inventory. This simply means that you will think about, admit to and write down, if possible, everything you have done to hurt yourself or someone else. A more detailed explanation follows, but know up front that the moral inventory is not intended to humiliate you and is not a tool with which to beat yourself up. When completed, the moral inventory will be a valuable tool for learning about yourself.

This Step is hard, and the next one is even harder, but I believe that if you do these Steps with an open heart and mind, you will be amazed at the change in your life. All the Steps are vital. None is more important than the other. However, consider the following. I was doing a series of meetings in the Montgomery County jail in Texas. Most of the guys at the meeting had attended many AA meetings before they got into jail. Some of them knew the AA literature and lingo and phrases better than I. I was very bothered by the fact that, although they knew AA and had attended AA meetings on the outside, they persisted in their lifestyles and wound up behind bars. When we got through the Twelve Steps, I could see some of the guys didn't relate to what I was saying, even though they said they knew the program. I asked the group of about twenty-two guys how many of them ever took the Fourth and Fifth Steps. *None* of them had!

Two weeks later, I was attending a meeting at the prison in Huntsville, Texas. We were going through the Steps at this meeting as well. Again, most of these guys really knew the program, and again, I was dismayed as to why men who could really get into the meetings and literature wound up in prison. I asked the same question, "How many of you took the Fourth and Fifth Steps?" Of the forty or more men there, only *one* had, and he wasn't in prison for an alcohol-related offence. This man was back in prison because of parole violations. He is out now, and I miss him, because he would tell the other guys that it was necessary to take all the Steps in their proper order, especially Steps Four and Five.

Surely these are not scientific polls, but they confirmed what I had heard over the years. My first sponsor, Hank, pushed me to do these Steps. I am not easy to push, but he didn't give up, and his persistence paid off for me. Thank you, Hank. I don't know how he got through to me; no one else had been able to do that except Dr. Mike. God put him in my life when I was somewhat willing and had the humility to reach out and to listen. Over and over again we see one alcoholic deliver God's message to the sick man. Hank was the messenger God put in my life; he was the one who encouraged me to complete this and all the remaining Steps.

So, if you want to stay in the program, if you are serious about getting sober, do all the Steps. Once you complete four and five, you will want to do the rest. You will get better, life will get better, and you will begin to know a God you don't want to live without. You will find moments of peace just being in His presence. Sometimes these moments are unbelievably peaceful. As a result of feeling His presence, you will want to rid yourself of any selfishness that stands between you and Him. As said before, selfishness and self-centeredness are the twin roots of our problem. As we write out the Fourth Step, we will see the selfishness of our ways and the patterns of self-destructive behavior that have ruled our lives to this point.

The *Big Book* has a wonderful way of laying out how to do Step Four. Read it and follow it as best you can. If you need other guides, there are all kinds available, but as a well-known athletic company says, "Just do it." Don't worry about doing it perfectly, just do it. The critical thing is that you pick up a piece of paper and a pencil and start. When faced with a blank sheet of paper you might find it hard to get started. Try just writing down your name, where you were born, how many brothers and sisters you have and so on. Write your earliest memories, good or bad, write about how you felt about your role in the family growing up. What in your life has made you angry, what mistakes have you made, who have you hurt, who has hurt you and how have you dealt with the hurt. Again, this is not a paper for your English teacher; you won't be graded on spelling or grammar. Don't look at this with dread as a task or a job; look at it as an opportunity to learn why you have lived the way you have lived. With this knowledge, you can recognize patterns and learn what you can do to change them.

A moral inventory is simply a history of our rights and wrongs over the course of our lives, so be prepared to write. If you put it on a computer, make sure it is password protected, because you will eventually spill your guts into this effort. If you can't protect your writing from others, make notes that only you will understand. If you are incarcerated, just be careful. However, do not use your circumstances as an excuse for not completing this Step.

Start from the beginning; remember back as far as you can. The things that stick in your gut will come to you. Those are probably the important things. No one cares when you learned to ride a bike, but it is important why you were angry with your father, mother, whomever. Write down the things you are embarrassed about. Write down the things you are ashamed of. Write down the resentments you have. Write down your fears. List those with whom you are angry. These are all clues to who you are.

Most alcoholics have a big store of resentments. Some may not be aware of them, but they are there and burning up soul power. We are told that if we don't rid ourselves of them, they will kill us. To resent something or someone is to have the ability to "re-feel" the same anger, fear, and hostility today for something that happened in the past, even twenty, thirty, or sixty years ago.

My mother and I really didn't get along well. She didn't like me, my behavior, or the wall I built to protect myself. She said some things over the years that were pretty brutal. She also had a great dislike for my Uncle Jim. One of the funnier things she would say to me while flailing at me when I pissed her off, and I seemed to do that a lot, was, "You are just like your Uncle Jim, you *&^*." She never knew I really liked Uncle Jim. I really didn't know what she was talking about; hell, Jim is a good guy.

If we can re-feel something that happened to us five, ten, or twenty-five years ago, it is like carrying around a sack of crap on our shoulders. Some of those sacks get real old, real heavy, and real stinky. The people who caused the resentment may not even know they did or may have forgotten about it completely. But we don't forget. We may forget physical abuse, but we will never forget the emotional and psychological abuse—the times we were called stupid, idiot, fatso, and all the other names that degraded us. We are determined that, damn it, we are going to keep this hate and anger going as long as we live. Hate and anger kill the soul. They are instruments of self-murder. When we wallow in resentment, we waste time and exhaust effort that has no result other than to add to the scars on our souls. It is sin, but in many ways it is what keeps us going. "I will never forgive or forget," becomes our unspoken motto. Today I know how poisonous those resentments are. God does forgive and does forget. Today I am glad of that. He forgives our trespasses as we forgive those around us. Forgive we will; forgive we must.

One of my old buddies, John H., long gone with close to forty-five years in AA when he passed, used to say, "Keeping resentment is like taking poison and expecting the resented person to die." Those I resent are sleeping well at night while I am here lying in bed, tossing and turning sleeplessly, hating them and wishing them evil. They sleep well while I am killing myself. Most addicts have great resentments that go back to our earliest days. They, in fact, started the wall-building. When they flare up, they can bring back the same, and sometimes even greater, anger as when they were first experienced.

I can't be a decent person or claim to love anyone, much less God, if I have all this poison festering in me. I have to get it out, just like any other infection. That is what this Step is about—lancing the infection and letting all the poison flow out and away.

As for fear, a lot of us big boy and girl addicts claim we don't have any fears. We act like we are too tough for that stuff. That kind of statement comes from many people who are new to the program. We cover up our fears, or maybe better said, we drink away our fears. When we begin to live in reality and make progress with the inventory, many of us will find our lives were run by fear. These are not rational fears like being afraid of skydiving for the first time (there will never be a first skydiving experience for me). These are irrational fears, not based in reality but phobias and self-manufactured fears. These fears are the ones we have in our heads. They come from the voices that are always telling us, "They won't like you," or "they are going to find out you aren't as brave as you pretend to be." The voices that say, "You have no abilities, you will never measure up, never succeed, never do things right." The messages we repeat to ourselves go on and on, and we get so caught up in seeing the negative side of things that our ability to see anything positive is diminished. As my friend Ajon used to say, "We become awfulizers." Fear causes us to see the negative outcome of most life issues, and we expect the worst.

I was deathly afraid of flying for many of the years that I had to travel. My sense of being unloved and unwanted as a child somehow translated into fear—especially when I wasn't in control. In my distorted reality, the more I drank the more skilled and experienced the pilots became. Well thank you, United Airlines pilots, for keeping me safe. The worst hasn't happened. Over the years I have flown well over a million miles and today, I don't need Jack Daniels to be my comforter.

Resentments and fears bring anger. When we display anger, it is usually much more than the situation warrants. Alcoholics live in an angry world. Our families and coworkers know it and head for the hills when we start to blow up. We are discontent, life is not working out the way we wanted, and our self-will is exhausted. We can't run the show. Our self-reliance has failed us. We are not getting our way, and the world needs to know that ours is the right way—the only way. Through completing my inventory, I learned that I can't take criticism, and I get angry if someone else is praised. It is the "what about me" stuff over and over again.

Until I wrote my inventory and began to see myself objectively for perhaps the first time, I didn't know why I was always so concerned with what others were doing or saying. I didn't know why I could never be "in the moment" and just enjoy life. I can remember standing in a beautiful trout stream in Wyoming. I was in a beautiful location, doing something I loved. The sun was shining in a clear blue sky and I was busy being mad at the world. Even in this idyllic spot, my mind was elsewhere. Rather than focusing on fishing, which was wonderful, I let my mind go all over the place, and most of the places it went were awful. Not until after completing this Step and working on the other Steps did I come to fully realize that I have the power to choose what I think about! My overwhelming preoccupation with myself and the protection of that self didn't allow me to enjoy the moment I was in. What a waste of time and life! The program teaches us to live one day at a time. Sometimes it is one moment at a time. It took me a long time to learn to enjoy what I am doing at the moment and not to be thinking about all the what ifs and the people I would like to smack upside the head.

When you are writing your inventory, let it all hang out. Don't be afraid to let the truth out. We are only as sick as our deepest and darkest secret. Put it all on paper. Keep in mind, however, that there is no perfect Fourth Step. Simply do the best you can, without hiding from the truth. Be honest. For many of us, that is a new concept because we have lied to most folks and to ourselves over the years. In the past, we have lied to protect that inner child, but that is no longer necessary. No one need see, nor should they, what you are writing. This exercise is between you and God. God already knows your history, and if you find a way to hide things from Him, you will be the first in history. For the guys behind bars, it may be impossible to write down your inventory, and you shouldn't unless you can be certain no one else will read it.

Starting this Step takes courage. By now you have agreed that you are willing to go to any lengths to get and stay sober. Now is the time to demonstrate that willingness. Think about it, pray about it, and ask for His courage and guidance. I hear over and over that once a person starts in earnest, it just flows. If you have questions, talk to your sponsor. Go to meetings where there are Step studies. Listen to how others have done their Fourth Step, and let it happen.

Putting this inventory on paper is a wonderful exercise. It will probably be the first time you have taken a true snapshot of your life: the good, the bad, and the ugly. Be comforted to know that your inventory is no better or worse than the rest of your AA fellows. Our individual actions may be different, but underneath it all we are *all* the same. That sameness is part of the power of the program. No longer alone, we find we have the courage and determination. If all the AAs with years of sobriety completed this Step, so can you. Take hold of their encouragement and experience. One of my early mentors, Ed M., told me AA has two supporting rails to hold onto—the Steps and the fellowship. Grab hold of both, and move forward with the best effort you can muster.

The rewards of this Step are wonderful. It is when the program and God really start to come alive in our hearts. Don't think you are different from all other addicts and try to skip this Step. You are not too good, nor are you too bad, to ignore this vital exercise. The consequences of skipping this Step are more drinking and more drugging, because the poison is still inside you. By now, please God, you want a better life, and the better life is worth whatever pain and aggravation you think this Step may cause you. When you are on the other side and it is done, you will rejoice because you have made a major move to sobriety, peace, and understanding. You are not the only beneficiary of this and the other Steps. The changes that will be apparent as a result of your doing them will bring relief and gratitude to those around you, and those folks deserve some peace.

Doing this Step requires a big act of humility. Taking the moral inventory is not easy, but your life may depend on it. At this point, when we see our lives on paper, we get scared and begin to believe we really messed up. When we see what may be pages and pages of ways we have been hurt and/or hurt others, the times we lied, stole, cheated or worse, we may start believing that we are hopeless. Just remember that nothing is hopeless for God. Just be willing and have the humility to take this and the next Step. There is nothing, let me repeat, *nothing* on your paper that someone else hasn't done too. We've all done some awful things, but we are not awful people. We can change, and life can be worth living. You are not alone. What you have just done is an act of humility, not humiliation. Humiliation is what started the wall building in the first place. Humility is truth, and it eliminates the need for walls. We can be who we are and be happy about that fact.

Step Four—Ask Yourself:

1. Did you finish the Fourth Step as best you could?
2. Were you able to identify the things that have caused you to drink in the first place (resentments, fears, anger, etc.)?
3. Have you selected the person with whom you will share your life story? If it's not your sponsor, who is it, and why isn't it your sponsor?
4. Have you scheduled your Fifth Step?

Step Five

Admitted to God, to Ourselves, and to Another Human Being the Exact Nature of Our Wrongs.

The *Big Book* makes a very clear statement regarding this Step: "If we skip this vital Step, we may not overcome drinking." Up to this point in our pursuit of the Steps, our work has been reflective—learning the program, who we are, and what we need to do to get sober. Now we go into action. The actions will help us to get right with God and ourselves, and then, in the following Steps, they will help us get right with our fellow man. In this Step, we are going to take the inventory we wrote in Step Four and share it with another human being.

Perhaps for the first time, we take ownership of our will, our lives, and who we are. We begin to own who we are and truly live what we have learned. Step Five will re-introduce us to the world—this time a real world, not some figment of our alcoholic imagination. We can begin to let go of the world of self-defense and wall building—in other words, our old ideas. We can begin the lifelong process of embracing life, our true self, and our God. The old idea of inferiority and the need to hide that inferiority is rejected. Our new idea is that we are good, accepted, and capable of doing good things.

The Fourth Step was hard. Step Five takes more courage, but the rewards are life changing. I put off my Fourth Step for almost a year because I knew there was a Fifth Step and I would be damned if I was going to tell anyone the truth I knew I would uncover in Step Four. In reality, we are damned if we don't complete this Step. I went to confession for years and listed my sins, but I never understood why I did what I did until I completed this Step. I never took responsibility for my actions. I could always justify everything into you, he, or they made me do it.

There is a saying in AA that has a particular meaning with regard to this Step: "Growth starts when blaming stops." I know that I never took blame for anything I did. I was merely responding to outside stimulus. My life was like a pinball in a pinball machine. Like the metal ball ejected from the chute, I bounced off cushions and springs and people and things, reacting to the bumps and hits along the way. I never saw any rhyme or reason to my life. I was simply reacting to the situations I confronted as the years went by. I never realized I was always defensive and attempting to protect that inner child. Because I was always protecting myself, nothing was ever my fault. I drank because I was misunderstood. I drank because others tried to tell me what to do. I drank because my job was so stressful that I deserved the break and my bosses didn't know what they were doing.

Whose fault was it that I was drinking? Everyone else's but mine. My justification in my own mind was, "If you had to carry the same baggage that I do, you'd have to have an escape too." We all come to AA believing we are the only ones who had a hard life, but we soon find out that we are not. So whose fault is it that we drink? Our own.

Who have you been blaming for your need to drink? Is it your parents because they didn't love you enough, they were mean or even abusive? Did they treat your brothers and sisters better than they did you? Is your drinking the fault of the neighborhood in which you were raised? Is it the fault of those kids who made fun of you because you didn't have everything they had, or laughed at your problems with reading, or made fun of your weight? You don't have to look very hard to find someone or something to blame. You can keep on blaming and keep wallowing in your hurt or you can be willing to see how your reactions to people, places and things have to change. It is up to you to quit blaming and start growing.

To complete Step Five, you need to select someone with whom you are comfortable and most importantly, someone you can trust to hold your deepest confidences. Once selected, tell him or her what you are about. If he or she is not in AA, be sure that he or she knows what you are doing and why you are taking this step. Men should choose another man in completing this Step, and women should choose another woman. The last thing you need to do is select the most attractive member of the opposite sex with whom to share your problems. That is a recipe for disaster.

When you are ready to proceed, promise yourself that there is nothing you will hold back. There is nothing you won't disclose truthfully. If you do hold back, the Step is probably going to be a waste of time. It doesn't have to be perfect; none are. Forget perfect. Perfect is God, and you ain't God. If you forget something or some event, you can always revisit it later. Take your time to be thorough. Don't hesitate to open every door. This is your chance to dump it all, so take it. Completing this Step opens the pathway to a new life, free of the demons that you have carried from childhood. This will probably be the first time you will see your past in true focus instead of through the haze of alcohol. You will find that, like the rest of us, you have done some awful things, and you will begin to recognize the things that you did were awful, but you are not.

As you go through your inventory, see if you can find any common threads that motivated you to act the way you did. Was there any connection between your anger, gluttony, and arrogance? If you did such and such, why did you do it? When you were angry, why were you angry? When you wanted to kill your boss, why? When you had had it with your spouse, why? When you finish, consider all the whys and see if there is not just one reason for all your transgressions. Then, when you have finished your analysis, make sure you do this same analysis with your sponsor. Have him or her help you find the common motivations and connecting threads that have run through your life.

Once you've completed the self-analysis in Step Four, it's time to admit to another human being the exact nature of the wrongs. Again, this person will probably be your sponsor or someone in AA. Don't be surprised if your misdeeds don't blow him or her away. Chances are your confidant has heard it all before or even done the same things. I selected a priest, Father Tom, to be sure there was secrecy. He had been in the program for many years and had heard more than his share of Fifth Steps. I got more than a little pissed at him, however. My man, while I was pouring out my life transgressions, sat at his desk clipping his fingernails. Didn't he know how damn important I was and how honored he should be that I had carefully selected him to hear my horrors?

What Father Tom did do was ask me over and over again, "Why did you do that?" Why did I get angry? Why did I lie? Why was I fearful? Why did I have resentments? The same pattern that developed in writing out the Fourth Step became totally obvious when I did the Fifth. There was nothing on that paper that didn't come back to selfishness. That frail little ego I had needed to protect at all costs was the starting point for all my actions. My selfishness was hidden in other names: pride, fear, envy, resentment, anger—all of them are expressions of self-centeredness.

I was selfish and self-centered. I wanted everything my way. I wanted what I wanted, and I wanted it now! And as much as I wanted, I wanted it without any concern for the wants and needs of others. I really didn't give a crap for anyone else or others' needs. I came to understand that I spent forty-four years protecting that unheard child within my soul. I wasn't cared for by others, so I would take care of my needs on my own. That needy little son-of-a-gun inside my head orchestrated the way I lived.

An example of that consuming selfishness? In the early 1980s when I lived in Colorado with my wife and three small children, we experienced an unusually heavy snowstorm. Immediately across the street from my home lived another alcoholic. We both knew we needed to get out through the snow to secure our liquor supply for the weekend. We worked together shoveling snow and putting chains on my car tires. After hours of work, we managed to get to the main street and went straight to the liquor store to secure our supplies. Neither of us bothered to ask our wives if they needed anything or if the children needed anything. We were completely focused on getting our booze.

Once I admitted that I was selfish and recognized why, I realized that I no longer had to be a slave to my self-defenses. I didn't have to live that way any longer. Those powerful words, "You don't have to live that way anymore," were spoken to me by a young lady named Ann at my second meeting in 1985. I thought then, "How the hell do you know how I am living?" But she did know. Now I do too. Those gremlins of being less than, being a second—or third-class citizen, that sense of being unheard, were unfounded. I am not less than; I am not unwanted, unloved, or unaccepted. I am a child of God, a part of AA, and accepted by both.

You have probably heard of, or seen, the movie *Pay It Forward*. When something good happens for you, you pay it forward by doing something good for someone else. Before sobriety, we were paying forward the misery of our lives. We were splashing it forward or dragging it forward out of the past, taking the ugliness of what happened to us and passing it on to those around us. Once we understand what we are doing, it is easier to ask God for the grace we need to stop our crap sharing.

When we finish this Step, there is usually a great deal of relief from the burdens of carrying that sack of junk (it is no longer crap, just junk) we had on our shoulders for all those years. Some people say it feels as if a life burden has been lifted off their shoulders. They feel refreshed and renewed. There is a clear answer to the drinking problem. Some get to what we call "the pink cloud," similar to a runner's high. Some are just glad to get it over with and are content to believe the relief will come as they progress with the Steps. The vast majority of us wake up the next day wondering where the guilt has gone. Our Higher Power has taken it. He knows how we have suffered and knows too well the suffering we have caused. He is more than willing to take our guilt so we may move on to a better life—a life of faith, service, and amends. That pink cloud will fade at times and grow stronger at times as the years go by.

When we have completed Step Five, we will have taken a very in-depth look at ourselves, probably deeper than we have ever looked before. We now know our shortcomings. We begin to understand that we have isolated ourselves from our fellows, believing we needed to protect ourselves. While this knowledge is helpful in understanding our motivation, especially motivations of being selfish, the knowledge will not fix the problem. Self-knowledge isn't sufficient to keep us from the next drink; only God is.

For sobriety to develop and mature, we need to continue the Steps, supported by the fellowship of AA and accepting of God's love and forgiveness. The need for meetings, in my book, never goes away. That is where God shows up for us and we need the constant reminder of where we came from and how He has acted in our lives. As we progress with some level of spiritual living, we will get out of sync with the rest of society. When I attend a meeting, even after twenty or more years of sobriety, I am again shown the path I should be following.

The *Big Book*, on pages 75 and 76, suggests that we take an hour after we complete this Step to review what we have done. It says, "We thank God from the bottom of our heart that we know Him better. Taking this book down from our shelf, we turn to the page which contains the Twelve Steps. Carefully reading the first five proposals, we ask if we have omitted anything, for we are building an arch through which we shall walk a free man at last. Is our work solid so far? Are the stones properly in place? Have we skimped on the cement put into the foundation? Have we tried to make mortar without sand?"

If we can answer to our satisfaction, we then look at Step Six.

Step Five—Ask Yourself:

1. With whom did you take the Fifth Step and when?
2. Can you say you held nothing back?
3. Do you understand what motivated your actions in the past?
4. Did you find any patterns in the way you have lived your life?
5. Do you understand what the *Big Book* says about selfishness and self-centeredness?
6. Did you have a spiritual awakening during the days and weeks after you took the Fifth Step?

Step Six

Were Entirely Ready to Have God Remove All These Defects of Character.

Now that we have completed Steps Four and Five, we have a better understanding of what we did in Step Three when we decided to turn our lives and our will over to the care of God. If you were like me, you probably had no real idea what your will and life were. After doing these Steps, we finally begin to understand who we are, what motivated us, and why we did what we did and wanted what we wanted.

In the previous two Steps we listed our character defects and our sponsor helped us see what was hidden in the blur of self-centeredness. We now see ourselves and our actions more clearly than ever before. We know we received the gift of sobriety only after admitting defeat and coming to believe in the power of God to act in our life. In that same humility, when the connection is open to God, we ask Him to remove our character defects.

I believe Step Six is the pinnacle of all the Steps. We have reached the point of readiness to have God remove our defects. The remaining Steps are to keep us in this state of readiness because that's what it's all about—always being ready for God to act. Looking at our past and admitting and acknowledging our character defects is the first part of the process. If we don't then ask God to take those character defects away, we may wallow in the same mess forever. We humbly ask God to remove our defects and lift us out of the muck we created.

Year after year, meeting after meeting, I hear people say, "I am working to remove defect x, y, or z." The Step doesn't say that at all. The Step is pretty clear; the removal of character defects comes from God. I had no more ability to remove my anger and pride than I did to remove my addiction to alcohol. Sobriety came only when I gave up trying, surrendered, and asked God for help. That is the same pattern we have to use for every character defect: drinking, drugging, anger, use of pornography or sex, gambling, or whatever crutch we have used. We must give up trying to fix it on our own, surrender to God, and ask Him to remove it. Getting on our knees, a physical position of humility and surrender may be a good practice for some of us.

At a meeting, I heard an attendee say she had discovered fifty-six character defects. What an inventory that! I couldn't come up with fifty-six names to attribute to my defects, and I don't know how anyone could tackle such a laundry list. I might even say that her effort was one of self-centeredness and arrogance because she was, in effect, saying that she was more important than everyone else because she was worse than everyone else and had the list to prove it. Anyone taking on the task of resolving such a list will grow weary of the effort and will probably conclude that this Step is too much and it just doesn't work. My simplistic approach of saying that character defects all fall under the heading of selfishness makes the task of staying ready and focused much easier.

Sometimes we enjoy one or more of our defects and don't want to let them all go. We may think we need to surrender the drinking, but our gambling problem isn't that bad. We may know we need to give up the drinking and the gambling, but we aren't ready to let go of pornography. Trying to hold on to any one of our defects that separate us from God only perpetuates the belief that we can satisfy ourselves. Only God can fill the hole in our soul that we have all experienced.

Outsiders sometimes label AA as a self-help group. Nothing could be further from the truth. AA is a God-help group, and humility is the key to opening our hearts to God's voice, love, forgiveness, and direction. Again, the removal of the defects doesn't come through our power but through God's. The harder we work on eliminating a defect from our lives, the more we depend on self-power. I know now with all certainty that for alcoholics and drug users, self-power does not work. Our self-power is exhausted and exhausting. We have run out of it, and every time we try to eliminate a character defect under our own power, we are setting ourselves up for failure. As my friend Father Tom used to say, "When the horse is dead, dismount." We have ridden the horse of self-will into the ground. It's dead, and it's time to get off.

Critics will say we have given up our will and self-confidence. We say, "Yes we have, and now we have God confidence and God power." That is spiritual living. What could be greater? It is not self-deception; it is the truth. We see it work every day, not only in the lives of the people around us but also in our own lives. Reliance on the highest power is surely better than reliance on self-power. Living in this manner is out of step with most of the rest of society, especially any society that is in the business of amassing power and wealth. Look around at society today, from business to politics to the entertainment world and even the religious world, power is the goal. It may last for a while but only for awhile. Those of us seeking a spiritual life seek to plug into infinite, everlasting, power.

While many in AA have real and vital spiritual experiences, as a rule God doesn't speak directly to us on a daily basis, but we have come to believe that He can and does speak to us through our fellows in AA. The gift of sobriety does come from God, but most of the time He has it delivered via a messenger. The gift truly comes from Him; if it had a return address, it would be His. But He uses the delivery service of our fellows in AA. Imagine how a self-focused alcoholic would react if he or she heard directly from God. What a mess that would be. But if we get this God gift delivered by a drunk, well then maybe we will accept it for what it is. God chooses an alcoholic, most of the time one in recovery, to deliver the package of sobriety. An alcoholic delivering the message of sobriety is doing God's work. He or she is not responsible for how that gift is received, just the delivery.

Many of us alcoholics and addicts have messed up our lives beyond anything but divine repair. Even those who have been strapped to a metal chair in jail at one time or another can become the messenger of God's grace. The transformation from pants-wetting, staggering, puking, belligerent, ugly drunk to messenger is a miracle. Miracles such as this happen when we are open and ready to accept God's help.

Over the years I've met many of God's messengers and Harry O. was one of them. He was a World War II navy veteran who had served in the Far East. While on night watch on shipboard, he would memorize and recite poetry to stay awake. He was able to recite those poems well into his eighties. After his service, he became a prominent lawyer. He wrote books and notes on the history of Iowa and Nebraska. Harry joined AA about the same time I did. We attended many of the same meetings. He became a truly God-filled man, and I learned a lot from him. I remember him talking about trying to tune God in, as if on a short-wave radio. You keep working the dials to reduce the noise level so the voice of God becomes audible. The tuning was an effort to reduce the amount of selfishness in one's life. Harry taught me to understand one of the purposes of Step Five was to be able to recognize when my old behavior was kicking in. Once recognized, I could change what I was doing or saying or the way I was treating people. While I did not have the power to remove my shortcomings, I could change my thoughts and my actions, just as Harry would change the dials on the radio.

The more we are tuned in, the more open we are to God's gifts. Another old friend used to say to me, "All is gift." John M. was a lot smarter than I, so I listened to him very carefully. Even though I thought he should have said AA was "a" gift, he kept just saying "gift." Now I know he was correct. The whole deal is a gift freely given by God.

So for us today, sobriety and life itself as now lived is "gift." Like any gift received, there probably should be one given in return as an expression of gratitude. Give the program away to others who need it as freely as it was given to you. We do that at meetings and elsewhere when we talk with, visit, or help our fellows. We try to serve as God's delivery people.

At a meeting I attended, a young lady told a wonderful story of the gift given and received. As is the custom in many meetings, each attendee has the opportunity to speak or not. A young mom related the fact that she had a real hard time getting out of herself. She said she really didn't like people very much and preferred being left alone. She recognized this attitude as one not helpful to newcomers to AA. She remembered reaching out to someone before, and it took a lot of effort. Well, it turned out the next young woman to speak was the newcomer to whom the young mom had reached out! The young girl thanked the young mother from the depths of her heart and cried tears of joy. The acceptance that was offered and received was a life-changing moment for the newcomer and a moment of rejoicing for those of us who witnessed it. The one reaching out probably saved the new girl's life. God shows up at meetings and gives gifts.

If we want to receive and pass on the gift of sobriety, we have to get ready and stay ready. My prayer today, is "Teach me, God, to stay ready." We do that by living the previous Steps. When we are in the flow of completing Steps Four and Five and move on to Step Six, our spiritual readiness can bring us to the point of God acting in our lives in the same way He did when we were ready to have Him remove the compulsion to drink. The gift came when we were humble and admitted our powerlessness. Our ongoing duty as we pursue the spiritual life is to stay as ready as we possibly can.

The remaining Steps, when practiced on a daily basis, keep us in that place of readiness. The spiritual moment of being entirely ready follows our confession with the person we selected to hear our Fifth Step. When we finish that hard and painful task, there is nothing left standing between us and our God. We are open to His grace, we ask His forgiveness, and we humbly ask Him to do what we cannot do on our own—relieve us of the bonds of selfishness and its manifestations in our character defects. We ask to be rid of our anger, fears, dishonesty, and infidelities, all the defects described as the seven deadly sins.

Step Six—Ask Yourself:

1. Do you believe that anyone but God can remove your character defects?
2. Have you asked for the willingness/humility to become ready?
3. Are you as ready as you can be?
4. Can you agree that it is necessary to maintain some state of readiness to live the program?
5. Do you believe you can be entirely ready?

Step Seven

Humbly Asked Him to Remove Our Shortcomings.

It is only logical to move right into this Step immediately after we complete the Sixth Step. If we are entirely ready to have God remove the shortcomings, now is the time to ask Him. There is no good reason to wait. We may never be this ready again. The sequence of Steps Four, Five, Six, and Seven is beautiful. Probably for the first time, we learn who we are, confess our faults, become ready to have God remove them, and then just ask Him, in a humble way to remove them.

I encourage the fellows I have worked with to do Steps Five, Six, and Seven in pretty rapid sequence. There is a spiritual crescendo. The buildup brings us to a humble pleading to our God to remove all the things that stand in the way of our knowing and serving Him more and more. I am amazed by this Step. We started taking these Steps because we couldn't stop drinking. And now, just some weeks or months after we started the process, we are asking God to directly act in our lives. And more amazingly, we expect Him to do so.

An outsider might ask, "What the heck does this have to do with drinking?" If you are an addict, you don't have to ask; you know. You know that this is probably your only way out.

We talked before about humility and its place in the Steps. When we find our right place with God, we have a new way of communicating with Him. There is no demand in the words of the Step. There are no excuses for what we did. We take ownership for what we have done, and we reach a point of willingness to have God work directly in our lives and at His pace, remove the behaviors that separate us from Him. Just weeks or months ago, we wallowed in the depths of addiction. Now we have found a Power strong enough to pull us out of our self-centered pit. We come to the realization that we want nothing to stand in the way of our relationship with God.

I don't remember much of what I was taught in my college logic class, but I do remember there are things called syllogisms, and they go something like this. Everything that has fins is a fish. My pet has fins, and therefore, it is a fish. Every man is mortal. Socrates is a man; therefore, Socrates is mortal. And again, every truthful being is humble. God is a truthful being; therefore, God is humble. Although God is victor, ruler, and King of kings, perhaps we alcoholics are better off trying to understand Him as humility. I can relate better to a humble God after taking the Steps. He is not insulted, disappointed, or angry with me but forgiving. As I seek His forgiveness, He doesn't see my past but my present; He sees not what I did but who I am. He wants me to be my real self, not a slave to my old idea of self-protection. He wants me to be totally reliant on His protection. I have broken all His rules, marched through life as if I were God, and dismissed Him as a helper of the weak, yet He still forgives me and brings me back to life if I sincerely ask for His help.

The prayer AA associates with this Step is found on page 76 of the *Big Book*, "My Creator, I am now willing that you should have all of me, good and bad. I pray now that you remove from me every single defect of character that stands in the way of my usefulness to you and my fellows. Grant me strength as I go out from here to do your bidding. Amen." My guess is that Saint Francis would find this prayer to his liking. Francis wanted the very same thing for himself—to serve God and do His will. This is no different from what the alcoholic or addict is seeking.

Maurice C.

We ask for strength only to do His bidding, not our own. We ask Him to remove especially the defects that stand in the way of our usefulness. If there is a major defect, as long as we do not want to hold onto it, it's likely He will remove it. However, there may be some defects God finds useful and will not take away. In the second book of Corinthians, the apostle Paul referred to a defect that was a "thorn in his side" that God did not take away. We are not asking God to make us perfect; we are asking Him to make us perfectly useful.

There is that age-old question, "What do you have if you sober up a horse thief?" The answer, "A sober horse thief." Well, horse thievery will probably stand in the way of your usefulness to Him and your fellows. He will take that glaring major defect away as well. The lesser defects—well, they don't seem to slip away too quickly. If there is a defect that is not removed, it may be there to teach us ongoing lessons in humility.

I know my major defect is selfishness. It surely has not been removed, but it is not as bad as it used to be. A fellow AA member in Nebraska publicly showed he had surrendered the defect of selfishness. He actually had a phrase put on his license plate, "Ub4me!" It's a simple message. If I had those words on my license plate, it might curb my aggressive driving. As we surrender our selfishness, our thoughts become less of us and more focused on others.

I attended a meeting in a small town in Texas. A regular member of the group, a man I never met, recently had heart surgery. As the meeting was about to begin, a discussion started as to how Dave was doing since the surgery. It was very obvious that the group really cared about him. None of the discussion was self-serving. The talk was just about his well being and what could be done to help him. The attendees acknowledged that their good thoughts and prayers were going his way. I saw firsthand a group who had moved from self-centered to others-centered.

The transformation that takes place in most people's lives after they surrender their defects to God is amazing. I took a liking to a very gruff, crude, and loud fellow early on in my attendance at AA meetings. I was quite like him, loud and gruff, and we understood each other very well. One day this man, Marv, took me to his synagogue to visit and to show me the Sacred Scriptures. He opened the tabernacle, removed the Torah, embraced it, and kissed it with great reverence. This was not the Marv who had had a pretty tough reputation. He was a changed—never perfect but a changed—man.

Marv sponsored a very successful businessman who was also in the program. This fellow was asked, as we all were from time to time, to speak at meetings. When he finished his comments at the first meeting at which he gave a talk, he came back to Marv and asked, "How did I do?" Marv looked at him with some disdain and answered, "Who gives a shit?" That comment was perfect coming from Marv. This story reminds us not to get too heady about spirituality and our attempt to get close to God. It's not our self-importance that impresses God; it's our humility.

Humility is a concept that doesn't make much sense to a lot of us, but remember that God does for us what we cannot do for ourselves. This is a continuing theme of all the Steps. Recently at a prison meeting, a thirty-seven-year-old man related his history. At age eighteen, he was sentenced to thirty years in prison. At age thirty-seven he was getting out because his life had changed. He is an unbelievable example of how God's mercy and forgiveness works. I encouraged him to continue to attend meetings upon his release, and he said, "Don't worry, my dad has fifteen years in the program, and he will take me to daily meetings." Changes like his are beyond happenstance and good luck. Nothing—nothing— could have changed him but the power of God. He has a right relationship with God and asked to have his major character defects removed, and I believe they have been.

In each of the stories, we witness people suffering from alcoholism move out of themselves and into the real world. Now they are dependent upon the true Spirit and not liquid spirits.

They prepared themselves to have God act in their lives and they asked Him humbly to remove the barriers between them.

Step Seven—Ask Yourself:

1. How do you define humility?
2. Is it possible for an alcoholic/drug addict to be humble?
3. Do you believe God will act to remove your defects?
4. Why is Step Seven the key to Step Eight?

Step Eight

Made a List of All Persons We Had Harmed and Became Willing to Make Amends to Them All.

This Step moves quickly because it flows directly into Step Nine. The easy part of the Step is retrieving the inventory you completed in Step Four. Using that inventory, you will make a list of everyone you have harmed. Then comes the part of the Step that may or may not be difficult for you—being willing to make amends.

You should not begin Step Nine, actually beginning to make amends, until you are willing in your heart and soul to make those amends. You may be ready as soon as you review your list, or you may need to spend time in prayer. You have heard what is called the Serenity Prayer that is used not only by AA but also by many seeking peace. The Serenity Prayer, found on page 41 of the *Twelve x Twelve* says, "God, grant me the serenity to accept the things I cannot change, the courage to change the things I can, and the wisdom to know the difference."

Not only should you be praying for your willingness, but you should also be praying for the people to whom you need to make amends. Pray that they will be willing to be open to your sincerity. Remember that this Step is not about you. Following is a wonderful poem that was reportedly found on the wall of Mother Theresa's home in Calcutta. The poem seems to be an adaptation of a poem originally written by Kent Keith in 1968. It reminds us that life is not always about outcomes but about trying.

DO IT ANYWAY

People are often unreasonable,
illogical and self-centered;
Forgive them anyway.

If you are kind,
people may accuse you of selfish ulterior motives;
Be kind anyway.

If you are successful,
you will win some false friends and true enemies;
Succeed anyway.

If you are honest and frank,
people may cheat you;
Be honest anyway.

What you spend years building,
someone could destroy overnight;
Build anyway.

If you find serenity and happiness,
they may be jealous;
Be happy anyway.

The good you do today,
people will often forget tomorrow;
Do good anyway.

Give the world the best you have,
and it may never be enough;
Give the world the best you've got anyway.

You see, in the final analysis,
it is between you and God;
It was never between you and them anyway.

By now you are getting more comfortable in your own skin. Rather than getting carried away with your newfound joy and sobriety, you need to take the time to bring to mind the people you have hurt while you were an active addict and/or alcoholic. Your joy should not block out the names of the people and the institutions you have hurt in the past. Make the list, give it careful consideration, and review it with your sponsor.

As the years go by, there is a very good chance names and situations will pop into your mind out of the blue. As time goes by you may see more clearly who you are and who you aren't. This Step and the next may be never ending and that's okay. As your sensitivity grows you may gain a deeper understanding of your actions and how you hurt the ones you loved. There is always time to right the wrong. When you are really willing to make amends, you are ready to move on to Step Nine.

Step Eight—Ask Yourself:

1. Have you made your list?
2. Is there anyone on the list who you are unwilling to approach?
3. Have you prayed for the willingness?
4. Have you prayed for the people you have harmed and asked God to open their hearts to your effort to make amends?
5. Are you ready to review the list with your sponsor?
6. Are you willing to listen to your sponsor's advice regarding your list?

Step Nine

Made Direct Amends to Such People Wherever Possible, Except When to Do So Would Injure Them or Others.

Making amends is one of the Steps you may have heard about before you even thought of joining AA. It seems to get the most publicity. An entire television series, *My Name is Earl*, revolved around the main character trying to make amends for all his past wrongs. Earl, however, was making amends to appease "karma," basically trying to use his own power to ensure himself a better future and a better life in the next go 'round.

Like Earl, many of us approach this Step as if it is a chance for us to unload all our guilt. If we approach the Step that way, we are going right back to being selfish; it's all about us. Our objective is to try to make right those wrongs we have committed. This is not to relieve our guilt; it is to get ourselves right with our spouses, our children, our employers, our neighbors, and anyone else we have harmed. For those of us in AA, making amends is about making others' lives better.

I believe the only way to get ready to make amends is through prayer. This Step takes an enormous amount of courage. Go to the source of the Power that lifted your drinking compulsion and ask Him to help you.

Our sponsors are of vital importance when taking this Step. We should still have the list of those we offended from completing Step Four, and our sponsor probably reviewed that list with us.

Counsel with him or her before you charge into this next Step. There is a wonderful account of a fellow doing this Step in the *Big Book*. He was one brave and courageous man. He stood up in church and began his amends in front of the entire community. Most of us won't have such courage and will be well advised to talk things over with our sponsor before our enthusiasm to make amends makes us charge off without thinking and praying.

When you think you are ready, role play and review the list with your sponsor before you begin. I could tell some horror stories about zealous members who plowed ahead before they knew what they were about. Some of them are lucky to still be married, and some are lucky to be alive.

Sponsors are vital in giving direction when it has to do with making amends to members of the opposite sex with whom you had a past relationship. There is no value, and potentially real harm, in inserting yourself into the present life of a past lover. He or she probably doesn't want to hear from you and probably doesn't want a current relationship to be impacted by your self-satisfying intrusion. If you feel a burning need to make amends to a former lover, try writing a letter to that person and then destroying it without mailing it; confess to your spiritual advisor or your sponsor. You may want to confess to God that you have this guilt and give it to Him.

I want to caution that some people to whom you feel you need to make amends might not want to hear it. They may want to deny that you ever even had a problem or try to brush it off as "no big deal." Again, it's not your job to convince them you did them harm. It's only your job to lay the amend at their feet and let them accept it or reject it as they see fit.

This Step says we made amends. Amend means make things right. It doesn't mean you take on the task of telling everyone you harmed, hurt, or stole from that you are sorry. While drinking, we used the word "sorry" to the point that it has no meaning when it comes out of our mouths. It is much more than being sorry. It's living a sober life in the real world and carrying through with the promises we have made every single day for the rest of our lives.

There are some amends we will never complete, but that doesn't mean we shouldn't start the process. Listen to your sponsor, and remember the Step says "all." That means everyone and every institution on the list. Again, keep in mind the idea is to make amends, not make things worse. A general announcement in the local newspaper will not do the trick. If you have taken something, return it. If you short-changed your employer, make up for it in any way you can. If you didn't pay your bills, pay them. Do it all with the advice of your sponsor.

For the majority of us, the amends will be mostly focused on our families. Our drinking and drugging had terrible consequences for them. By fulfilling our self-serving addictions, we ignored, abandoned, and probably treated those closest to us horribly. We repeated the same patterns and attitudes of our parents or caregivers who damaged us. We passed along the same old sick treatment we learned to the ones who should be the most precious to us. At no other place more than home is the word "sorry" meaningless. We wore that word out years ago as the family saw us go from "sorry" to the bottle time after time. This time, however, is different. This time we have AA to lean on for support. This time we will prove it by staying sober today, the next today, the next today, and so forth.

Be aware that while you are excited about your newfound life and are eager to make changes, some members of your family might not be ready or willing to go along with your new plan. A spouse who has spent years hiding your indiscretions or who has, by default, been the head of the family may find it difficult to let you take the reins back. A child who has missed you at school programs, ball games, or performances may take awhile to join in your excitement. All I can advise is to keep living your amends and pray for open minds and hearts.

The best amend we can make is living a life of sobriety and showing our family the unconditional love and acceptance we have found. By introducing them to what we are learning and living through AA, we can show them that they were not, and are not, the cause of our bad behavior. The last thing we want to do is leave them with even the smallest thought that they could have cured us. We can teach them that they do not have to follow our path, and perhaps, by doing that, we can break the chain that has bound our family, perhaps for generations. If there is one hope shared by many of the prisoners I meet with, it is that they have the opportunity to end the pattern of pain and suffering that has been passed down in their families for generations.

The miracles that occur in families as a result of these living amends are unbelievable. Sons and daughters moved from having hate for their alcoholic parent to being grateful, forgiving children. Spouses can get back together. Siblings can reunite and grow supportive of the sick family member and encourage each other as no other can in the life of sobriety. Grandparents are allowed to see and even care for grandchildren. Trust is re-built and promises kept. Families become whole again. Over and over again we hear of mothers being reunited with their daughters and sons and fathers and children coming together after years of separation. The blessings of seeing a father reunite with his son or a mother with her daughter are proof of God's power working in the program.

There are, however, occasions when family is lost for good. Don't blame the family. They were not the addicts; they were not the bad actors. There is nothing sadder than an inmate who is abandoned by his family, never visited by a wife, son, or daughter. But if the family is lost beyond repair, use the fellowship of AA as your new family, and rejoice in that. Live the life of sobriety with your AA fellows. Make your life amends in any way possible to make yourself of maximum service to God and the people around you, even if the new life is without your physical family.

There are times when the people we most need to make amends to have passed on. I have seen several ways AA members have still done their best to make amends to these people. Sometimes it is through prayer, sometimes a letter written to the deceased, and sometimes a visit to a gravesite. Again, living the life God meant you to live will be the best amend you can make.

As you work through your amends, you will be amazed when you feel what AA calls "a new freedom and a new happiness," and that is the truth. I have found the promises listed in the AA literature to be true in my own life as I have worked through the Steps. I have given up all hope for a better past. My horse of self-will has died, and I have dismounted. The God who shows up at meetings is more and more in my heart and actions. He is doing things for me that I never even considered, much less thought possible. I have given up fighting life and have received blessed peace. While I realize that being relieved of my self-centeredness will be a lifelong project, I can claim that I am not quite as arrogant or as much the selfish butthead I used to be.

These same promised gifts—peace, serenity, loss of self-centeredness, and dumping the load of crap we have carried for so long—are there for every alcoholic and/or addict who accepts them.

If this is your first time through the Steps, you will have grown into a better and more productive citizen of the world. When you become a sponsor, you will go through this process with the person you sponsor and will see and understand even more. That will be true the next time and the next time and the next time. You can look forward with anticipation to a deeper understanding each time you go through the Steps.

Step Nine—Ask Yourself:

1. Are you fully aware that making amends is not for your benefit but for the benefit of the other person?
2. Have you started making your amends?
3. Is there anyone to whom you are reluctant to talk?
4. Is there anyone you cannot make amends to? If so, have you considered writing him or her a letter?
5. Have you begun making restitution where possible?
6. What's the difference between sorrow and amend?

Step Ten

Continued to Take Personal Inventory, and When We Were Wrong, Promptly Admitted It.

Whew! We've made it through nine Steps. We've given up alcohol and drugs, we've gotten right with God, and we've done our best to make amends. We're done! Right? That may be the temptation—to believe that our work is done. The truth is, Steps Ten, Eleven, and Twelve are necessary to keep us always ready, to keep us on the spiritual path set out for us, and to help us continue to receive the gifts and pass them on.

Step Ten acknowledges our frailty as human beings. As much as we would love it, we are not fixed. Drinking is truly not a problem for us any longer. Would that the same was true for our character defects. Some of them, especially those that separate us from God, are diminished, but we are still and always human. We will continue to make mistakes, but we will no longer use alcoholism as an excuse. We want to move forward on our spiritual path, and to do so, the daily personal inventory is most helpful.

Over the years, I have heard many people recount how they do their inventory. I know only one—and there are probably many more—who does it daily according to the *Big Book*. Every evening, Dave takes out his pad and pencil and reviews his day. He jots down things important to him. He gets to see daily where his selfishness is showing up. He looks not only at what he could have done better; he looks at what he did well. He knows where his Higher Power is helping him and is thankful for that reality.

When we first read this Step, it is gratifying to see the word "when" not "if." Remember, we are not saints, but we can claim spiritual progress. Making this inventory and reviewing it becomes a great prayer time. Time to thank God for His help and ask for the help we need. For most, the drink problem has been removed, and we are living in a safe place. But to keep safe, we are told to continue the spiritual journey. One of the, if not the, best admonitions we learn from the *Big Book*, page 85, is, "We are not cured of alcoholism. What we really have is a daily reprieve contingent on the maintenance of our spiritual condition." Doing a personal inventory helps us stay in that place of humility where God is active in our lives.

All during our drinking days we existed by forcing our will on the world and those around us. Our willpower didn't work, and now we have a Power that does work. If we take all the willpower we have and align it with God's will, we are finally lining up with life. Not only is God on our side, but we are on His. This becomes a great source of peace for us. Sometimes that peace fills us until we tremble. Sometimes God speaks with a loud voice, and He is most audible when we continue to be ready to have Him remove our defects.

The faithful use of this Step keeps us current in our inventory. We identify those things in our character that need immediate attention. We don't wait to address those we wrong. We go to them promptly and admit our mistakes. By staying current, we avoid the building of anger and resentments. By staying current, there is no need, unless you want to, to repeat Steps Four and Five again. Some people, as part of spiritual exercise, find it useful to repeat from time to time their Fourth and Fifth Steps. That is a personal decision and made with the advice of a sponsor.

I've been reminded by one of the gentlemen that I've had the honor of sponsoring, "We should stop being surprised by our stupidity." We never lose the ability to do wrong. In the early years, I was surprised when I messed up. I used to get shocked and say, "Holy—, I did it again." Today messing up is no longer a surprise and it is easier to admit my wrongs. I do see a small change in my thinking however, now when I screw up I tend to be more concerned for the one I've offended than to be surprised at my humanity.

According to the *Big Book*, page 84, "We have entered the world of the Spirit. Our next function is to grow in understanding and effectiveness. This is not an overnight matter. It should continue for our lifetime. Continue to watch for selfishness, dishonesty, resentment and fear. When these crop up, we ask God at once to remove them. We discuss them with someone immediately and make amends quickly if we harmed anyone. Then we resolutely turn our thoughts to someone we can help. Love and tolerance of others is our code."

We incorporate Steps Four, Five, Six, Seven, Eight, and Nine into our daily lives, doing our best to stay in that state of readiness that opens our hearts to His action. When we live this way, "We have ceased fighting anything or anyone—even alcohol. For by this time sanity will have returned." (*Big Book*, page 84-85) Sanity, that state of being we sought in Step Two, is returned to us. Our lives have changed. We are no longer the victims of wall building. We become free and unshackled by anything, especially alcohol. The discussion for Step Ten continues: "We felt as though we had been placed in a position of neutrality—safe and protected. We have not even sworn off. Instead, the problem has been removed. It does not exist for us. We are neither cocky nor are we afraid. That is our experience. That is how we react so long as we keep in fit spiritual condition."

As we review our inventory on a regular basis, we become more aware of the decision we made in Step Three to turn our will and life over to the care of God. We see that we have changed from self-serving to God-serving and serving God's children. Sobriety has not brought an end to our life problems, but it has provided us a system for dealing with those problems. We are no longer victims but are on a path that acknowledges our lives are in His hands and He continues to do for us what we cannot do for ourselves. As problems arise, and they surely will, we won't depend on a flimsy wall of self-protection but on a solidly built foundation. Our foundation is built on a Power who can carry us through any difficulty. We are not alone, and if we continue to rely on that Power, we will never be alone.

Step Ten—Ask Yourself:

1. Do you take the time to complete a regular, even daily, inventory?
2. Does the inventory help you identify areas that you need to turn over to God?
3. Does your inventory remind you of your need for dependence on your Higher Power?
4. Are you serving others?

Step Eleven

Sought Through Prayer and Meditation to Improve Our Conscious Contact With God, *as We Understood Him,* Praying Only for the Knowledge of His Will for Us and the Power to Carry That Out.

So many times newcomers wonder what God's will for them might be. They wonder if they will have to go to mission lands, take vows, or do something dramatic. That is self-focus: What do I have to do? Where do I have to go? God's will is for us to help each other get through life with some peace and joy and to acknowledge Him. The spiritual life then seems as simple as trying on a daily basis to do His will and to serve as best we can our fellow man as He puts them in our lives. There is no magic and no heroism. We are just trying to be nice human beings who are honest with and caring toward our fellows and confident in God's protection.

For those seeking to know what God's will for them might be, consider this. Don't get drunk. Seek help if you have a problem. Imitate the people who, with whatever help, have overcome their addiction. Do something good for another human being. Learn to pray, and attempt to be humble. Be honest. Put other people's needs first.

The words of this Step assume that we have a conscious contact with God. We go about the day asking His direction and thanking Him for the grace of sobriety. We are encouraged to deepen that contact through prayer. Some people believe that they are not worthy, that God does not want to hear from them. They may believe that prayer is only for holy folks. Holy folks are really those people who truly understand their unworthiness and know that God wants to hear from them. Prayer is for everyone, everywhere, in every situation. We are now on a relentless journey to do His will. We are reminded that praying for our own goals and the satisfaction of our needs is set aside while we pursue His will for us. I believe His will for me is that I be available to help my fellows get through life because sometimes life is very difficult and we need all the help we can get. I also believe He wants me to accept the reality that I am just as He wants me to be. I pray for the day when I absolutely live the reality that if I'm good enough for God, I'm good enough for me.

One of my quirks is that if I see a penny on the ground, I pick it up because it has a special meaning for me. I remember my grandmother telling me stories she heard as a young woman in Ireland. One story was that there was so much money in the States, if someone dropped a coin, they didn't even bother to pick it up. My family and friends laugh at my penny quest, but I've always gotten a small thrill out of finding a penny just lying there on the ground, waiting for me to find it. Picking up the penny has become even more significant for me. As the years have gone by, each time I get the impulse to do something out of the norm of ordinary kindness, I always question whether I should do it and ask God for the penny sign. I almost always get the sign and my wife smiles when she sees me stoop down to pick up a penny because she knows I will soon be up to something.

I am sure it is God's will that we do not drink. I believe it is His will that we take and then live as best we can the Twelve Steps. I believe it is His will that we attend meetings, pray, and stay in touch with AA and our sponsors. I believe it is His will that we take care of one another, that we are loving and tolerant, and that we share the gift of sobriety. There is a Latin phrase, *"Nemo data quod non habet."* It means, "You can't give what you don't have." I believe it's also true that you can't keep what you don't give. We should seek out opportunities to share the program with those who need it. If some get special graces to do special things, God bless them. Remember, this is a spiritual journey, and only God knows where He wants to take you.

I love to go to meetings where the Eleventh Step is discussed because I am anxious to hear how others employ this Step in their lives. My good friend Father Tom told me, "There is no such thing as a bad prayer." Some of us think we have to do this "right" or it is a waste of time. I agree with Tom. Anytime we direct our thoughts and focus on God is time well spent unless we are praying for Him to bring evil on someone else. It doesn't have to be long or complicated or according to the book. In the Bible, referred to by the founders of AA as the other big book, Jesus told His followers to not be like the hypocrites who think long-winded, fancy prayers are heard by the Father. He also told His followers in Matthew chapter six, verse six, that, when they pray, they should not stand on the corner speaking for other people's benefit but go into their closets to pray. Prayer is just between you and God. We can't impress Him even if we try. He knows who we are better than we know ourselves. I believe He is just glad to hear from us.

You may hear someone say at a meeting, "Don't think, just do." While that advice may be well motivated, I believe it's mistaken. As we begin to understand the program, our thinking changes. One of the biggest gifts we receive from God is the ability to think. It's what distinguishes us as humans from the rest of creation. It is impossible not to think; no matter what you are doing, you are thinking about something. The focus should be on keeping your thoughts going in the right direction. It's not the thinking that's bad; it's the wrong thinking. That being said, when it comes to prayer, don't over-think. Don't spend your prayer time worrying that you are not saying the right words or saying the words in the right order. God does not care if you have a degree in English, philosophy, or theology; He cares that you want to talk to Him.

If you are new to prayer, you may perceive your Higher Power as some being far, far away. Perhaps you can learn from the exercise I was taught by one of the inmates at the Wynne Unit. At our AA meeting, we were discussing the closeness of God to each of us. This inmate suggested that we close our eyes and place the palm of our hand in front of our face, as close as we could without touching our nose. After a few seconds he told us to open our eyes and notice that all we could see was our hand. He said that God is even closer to us than that. Thank you B.C.

Prayer is so important for spiritual growth, yet some of us avoid it because we think we don't know how to pray. Many of us revert back to prayers we learned as children, and that is wonderful. After all we have gone through, we probably know now how beautiful those old prayers are. The prayer of Saint Francis is quoted in the *Twelve by Twelve* on page 99. That prayer says, "Lord, make me a channel of thy peace—that where there is hatred, I may bring love—that where there is wrong, I may bring the spirit of forgiveness—that where there is discord, I may bring harmony—that where there is error, I may bring truth—that where there is doubt, I may bring faith—that where there is despair, I may bring hope—that where there are shadows, I may bring light—that where there is sadness, I may bring joy. Lord, grant that I may seek rather to comfort than to be comforted—to understand, than to be understood—to love, than to be loved. For it is by self-forgetting that one finds. It is by forgiving that one is forgiven. It is by dying that one awakens to Eternal Life. Amen."

When I was a child in parochial school, I learned that prayer is the act of lifting our minds and hearts to God, and we can do that in countless ways: reading prayer books, certain prescribed prayers, walking on a beach, observing God's creation in nature, looking at a new grandchild. In simple terms, it means taking a break from thinking about ourselves and focusing our thoughts on our God. Prayer is feeding time for our souls. By placing our focus on God, our souls are fed. When we go to God to praise or thank Him or ask His aid for others, we receive the Spirit and the strength to further seek His will. Don't forget that one of the greatest gifts humans have been given is the ability to decide what we want to think about. We get to choose the thoughts we hold onto. The more we choose to acknowledge Him, the more we open the window of humility, God's playground.

Many meetings conclude with the recitation of the Lord's Prayer. I think the words of that prayer express the true meaning of the Steps. Most people know the words to that prayer, found in Matthew, chapter six, verses nine to thirteen, "Our Father, who art in Heaven, hallowed be thy name. Your kingdom come, your will be done, on earth as it is in Heaven. Give us this day our daily bread, and forgive us our trespasses as we forgive those who trespass against us. Lead us not into temptation, but deliver us from evil. For thine is the kingdom, and the power, and the glory forever and ever. Amen." We can take that prayer into a meditation.

Rather than simply saying the words, we can stop after each phrase and really dig into what the words mean. What does Father mean to you? How can you make His name holy? What does it mean for His kingdom to come? What is His will? Let your mind go into the words and seek their deeper meaning, and then let inspiration come back to you. After reviewing the words of the Lord's Prayer, consider as well the words of the prayer of Saint Francis. Both of these prayers are a great starting place for all of us. We pray for His will to be done. We learn our forgiveness is linked to the forgiveness we offer others and that the kingdom, the power, and the glory are all His, not ours.

In parochial school, I was taught that there are basically three kinds of prayer we can offer. The first type is petition and then thankfulness and adoration. In our prayers of petition, we are asking God for something. We have learned by now that we do that humbly, focusing on the needs of others. We ask; we don't demand. There are really three responses to our petitions: yes, no, and not yet. Sometimes our requests are granted readily, sometimes they are delayed, and sometimes they are never granted. It is up to our Higher Power to deliver what He thinks is best for us. We just ask as humbly as we can, leave the result in His hands, and accept the results we are given. The program teaches us to ask not for ourselves but for others. We are told to pray for the knowledge of God's will for us and the power to carry it out. We are not to pray to carry out our own will. There should be no more, "This is what I want, so give it to me" prayers. Our job is to pray, not to dictate what we think we need or want. The outcome of all our efforts is left in God's hands. This is the position of humility that tends to keep us ready to have God work in our lives.

Prayers of adoration are pretty simple. We simply appreciate God for being God. He is the beginning and the end. He is the Creator, He is the granter of gifts, especially sobriety, to us, and we recognize Him for who He is—God. The more beautiful and exciting our understanding of Him is, the more we will want to adore Him. He is the cause of the million miracles we see in AA every day. Sit, or better yet, kneel in adoration of Him who so cares for us. Just be at peace. Just be in love with your God.

The easiest prayer for the recovering alcoholic is the prayer of thanksgiving or gratitude. Once we receive the gift of sobriety, a thank you jumps out of our hearts. The relief we experience, the health we feel, and the recovery we have bring us our most natural response of gratitude. I love to go to so-called gratitude meetings. The witness that attendees offer is wonderful. They tell what life was like, what happened, and how they are now. The stories of miracles are repeated over and over again. To meet a man who was twenty years in prison in administration segregation who today thanks God for his sobriety is unbelievable. There are stories of young women who get their children back and men who get out of jail and devote their lives to the program—miracles all. I heard just recently a fellow, an ex-con, say, "If I am grateful to God for what I have through the program, I can't get drunk." I think he is correct.

If AA had a group holiday, it would be Thanksgiving Day. I hope that one day we can all answer like a convict I know who, when asked how he is doing, answers, "I am blessed and highly favored." Anyone who experiences long-term as well as short-term sobriety can't help but be thankful—thankful the fighting against life is over and that they recognize a new acceptance from the Higher Power and a fellowship that shows the way to God. We talk also at meetings about gratitude lists. My sponsor asked me to write one during my early days. I didn't know what he meant. I believed that everything I had, I earned. I didn't need to be grateful to anyone or anything. My ego prism was so self-focused it was burning a hole in my heart. My self-focus was so intense that I couldn't see beyond my own footprint. Thank God I don't have to live that way anymore.

Today, if I were to sit down and write a gratitude list, there wouldn't be enough paper on my desk to enumerate all I have to be thankful for. God has blessed AAs with life again, a real, loving, giving, and full life. These gifts are given through His generosity. Nothing we did earned them. They are gifts unmerited and undeserved. There is a practical side to focusing our thoughts on gratitude. It is impossible to be angry, fearful, or resentful if we are in a place of gratitude.

Thank you, God. I have heard hundreds of sermons over the years. I don't think I ever heard a preacher say that it is a good idea to thank God for being God. One of my Baptist buddies told me that I've just been going to the wrong church all these years. I think thanking God for being God is a great idea. My days are best lived when I am in the place of gratitude. So thank you, God, for just being You. You have a heck of a show, and I am grateful I found my place in it. Thank You!

At meetings, we hear great advice on developing a way of moving from prayer to meditation. In meditation, we take the time to listen rather than just talk. We fix on a thought that carries our mind to God and try to just stay there. Saying a simple prayer over and over again usually works for me. In the Eastern

Orthodox tradition, there is a wonderful short chant: "Holy God, holy, mighty one, have mercy on us." Another is, "This is the day the Lord has made. Let us be glad and rejoice." Consider various phrases from the Lord's Prayer or from the prayer of St. Francis, "Lord, make me a channel of Your peace." Repeat that simple thought over and over. The words of an ancient Latin hymn can still bring peace today, "Where charity and love prevail, there God is always found." Find or develop a short phrase you can repeat over and over, a mantra that puts you in His presence, and just stay in that presence. "Where charity and love prevail, there God is ever found. Brought together by His love, in love we are bound."

You might be surprised to know how often the subjects of God and prayer come up between prisoners. Some men in prison know prayer well. They know how to hook up with their God and how to stay in His presence. They come to peace with who they are and their need for forgiveness and acceptance of their shortcomings. They can be "into" God in the midst of all the noise and horror of living behind bars. Prayer and then meditation give them the opportunity to connect in a real way with their Higher Power and it becomes a true escape for them from the harshness of prison life. They know He wants to connect with them more than they want to communicate with Him. They know His power; they have experienced that infinite love. I am not talking about what some call the prison conversion or a conversion of convenience to accelerate their release but a true change. They are new men, and they live the life of the new man. They are daily examples to their fellows behind bars and they have served as God's messengers to me.

Step Eleven—Ask Yourself:

1. Do you find time every day for a few moments of prayer?
2. Can you say that your prayers are said for the well-being of others and not for selfish motives?
3. Do you believe that prayer works?

4. Do you believe that praying shows you know God is in your life?
5. Do you believe that prayer and meditation bring you closer to God and God closer to you?

Step Twelve

Having Had a Spiritual Awakening as The Result of These Steps, We Tried to Carry This Message to Alcoholics, and to Practice These Principles in All Our Affairs.

You will see that Step Twelve can be broken down into three parts: 1) We acknowledge we have had a spiritual awakening; 2) we agree that it is our privilege to be God's messengers in taking the program to other alcoholics; and 3) we agree that the principles of AA need to be part of our everyday lives. Let's look at each of these components separately.

The result of working the Steps is a spiritual awakening. We are not promised new spouses, new jobs, new health, new cars, or new homes. The only promise is a spiritual awakening. Having woken up spiritually, we are now living on a plane where we put God's will and care for our fellowman ahead of our own self-will and care.

Perhaps for us in AA a spiritual awakening has two key elements. The first is that God can do for us what we cannot do for ourselves, and the second is that we are attempting to live a more selfless life. By doing both, we place ourselves in the path of God's grace and aid. We are not saints. We are not perfect and never will be. However, we have been told by our founders that we are to grow along spiritual lines, to claim spiritual progress, and that the maintenance of our sobriety is contingent upon our spiritual condition.

As we live the Steps, we've gotten to know our real selves, we're comfortable in our own skin, and we are square with God and our fellows. We believe that God accepts us unconditionally. We know our fellows in AA accept us for who we are, and we are learning to accept ourselves as being just the way God wants us to be. The spiritual awakening we have experienced has nothing to do with the hallucinations or wild imagination we may have experienced under the influence of a mind-altering substance. It is real, it is practical, and we know it works.

The second part of Step Twelve says that we will make a real effort to share the gift we've been given and spread the message that AA is available to anyone who wants it. We want to reach out to our fellow alcoholics in meetings, treatment centers, halfway houses, prisons, jails, or on any occasion when we encounter someone suffering from the addiction of alcohol or drugs. We have found that the best way to keep the gift of sobriety is to share it. We know we can only carry the message; we can't carry the alcoholic. We have no desire to be more than who we are. We are not gurus or leaders or any more special than any of our fellows in AA. We count all our gifts and blessings as coming from God.

We are encouraged to share our stories with newcomers. Because we have been there and done that, we can probably relate to people seeking recovery better than anyone else in their lives. When we share our experiences, we let newcomers know that they are not alone and that they are not the only ones who have done whatever it is they have done. Our goal is to be a friend who may become a confidant or even a sponsor. We don't put obstacles in the newcomer's way by preaching to them. We just talk and encourage. We attempt to be a living example of what life without drink and/or addiction can be.

At one of my regular meetings, a young woman stood up in front of a group of more than 180 alcoholics. She was shaking as she said to the group, "I need help. Please help me." This act of humility opened a new world for her.

I promise you that when you reach out to others, you get to watch the miracles. You will watch people come back to life. You will see them reach out to their fellow alcoholics and become part of a wonderful fellowship with true friends. The reality of having true friends may be new to some of us. While we were practicing alcoholics, we didn't make friends; we took hostages. In our previous relationships, we wanted to control and manage how our friends treated us. We wanted them to make us the center of their lives. We needed them to love us to the exclusion of all others. Now we have the ability to make true friends— people for whom we truly care and who truly care about us and our wellbeing. We find ourselves in a community with common goals and the support and encouragement we may have never experienced before.

The lessons of this chapter will be well remembered every time we meet a prospect or participate at our regular meetings. The first lesson is that we will not place obstacles in newcomers' lives. They are already feeling embarrassed, confused, and probably fearful. It is our job to welcome them. It is not our job to smack them upside the head with rude or domineering language. Most newcomers are tired of being told what to do and don't want to be disrespected by being treated like children who don't know any better. The concept of disrespect is very evident in the prison system. The consequences of disrespecting a fellow inmate can be lethal.

We are honest and gentle but don't shy away from the principles of the program. We deliver the message of sobriety, but we can't confer it. We try to deliver it in a way newcomers can most readily accept it. We talk of how AA has affected our lives. We talk of the fellowship AA members enjoy. We talk, we listen, and we listen some more. We encourage. It is always our hope that the newcomer, when ready, will take the hand of God and with our encouragement, move to a life of sobriety. If the newcomer doesn't accept you or AA, move on, remembering him and all who still suffer under the lash of alcoholism in your prayers. Give the new person the *Big Book* and the *Twelve by Twelve* and simply say, "Read these."

While reading a short story about Mother Theresa, I learned a great lesson. She saw herself as a "Pencil in His hand." If that were me, I know that I would rather have reported that I was, indeed, the hand of God. That tells you where my humility is! What greater gift do we receive in our sobriety than to be the passageway from God, the pencil to show the way to our fellow sufferers? The following words are from a poem attributed to Mother Theresa in the book *The Blessings of Love*, published in 1996:

The very fact that God has placed a certain soul
in our way is a sign that
God wants us to do something for him or her.
It is not chance;
It has been planned by God.
We are bound by conscience to help him or her.

Once we take our eyes away
from ourselves, from our interests,
from our own rights, privileges, ambitions—
then our eyes will become clear
to see Jesus around us.

Keep the joy of loving Jesus
in your heart
and share this joy
with all you meet especially your family.

As we complete the Steps, we are encouraged to become a sponsor for someone else. As we walk through the Steps with someone else, our own spiritual awareness becomes stronger. When another alcoholic leans on us, we learn to lean harder on God and again acknowledge that God has done for us what we could not do for ourselves. It is a marvelous experience to see the person you sponsor become your teacher. God helps those we sponsor move beyond anything we have to offer.

Part three of Step Twelve says that we attempt to practice the principles of AA in all affairs. So what are the principles we will live by? We will be honest—this means we will tell the truth all the time, not just when it's convenient or serves our purpose. As children, we learn to lie because we learn that the chances are if we tell the truth we will be punished, but if we lie we may get away with something and skip the punishment. We may have even made a conscious decision to lie to avoid punishment. As alcoholics or addicts, lying became part of our everyday lives and may have become such a habit that telling a lie was easier than telling the truth. Now we have consciously made the decision to attempt to tell the truth at all times in all things.

In living the principles, we accept what we've been taught in the Twelve Steps. One thing we in AA say, "When we screw up, we 'fess up and no longer have need to cover up." We spend time each day in prayer in an effort to grow closer to our Higher Power. We come to depend more and more on His power and less and less on our own. We know the horse of self-will is dead, and we have dismounted.

We are grateful for what we've been given and what we've learned. We acknowledge our Higher Power and are content with our lot in life. We don't need or want to be anyone but ourselves. We know for a fact that there is no problem that drinking won't make worse.

Is the life of sobriety worth the effort of taking the Steps? For those of us who have taken them, the answer is a simple and resounding yes! None of us who have been blessed with sobriety wish to return to the world of lying, belligerence, unfaithfulness, sneakiness, anxiety, greed, and anger. There are those who come into AA and then, for whatever reason, go back to drinking. I have never heard one of them who subsequently returned to AA say they were happy while they were drinking again.

When we've completed the Twelve Steps with our sponsor, we've just begun. Now we attempt, some days feebly, some days with more vigor, to live what we have learned. Jump at the chance to sponsor someone else and keep the chain of love and acceptance growing. Oh yeah, keep going to meetings. Remember, that's where God shows up.

Step Twelve—Ask Yourself:

1. Are you incorporating the principles of AA into your daily living?
2. Are you working to improve your spiritual life by daily praying, acknowledging your faults, and asking God for help?
3. Are you participating actively at your meetings and providing service to your group?
4. Have you reached out your hand to a newcomer?
5. Have you gone out of your way to participate at meetings in halfway houses, prisons, jails, or hospitals?
6. Have you had the privilege of sponsoring anyone?
7. Have you helped someone work through the Steps?

AA in Jail and Prison

While living in Texas, I met two fellows who invited me to attend AA meetings behind the doors of the local jail and the bars of a nearby prison. Over the last four years, I have had the good fortune of being able to attend AA meetings in Montgomery County Jail on Tuesday evenings and at the Wynne Unit Prison in Huntsville, Texas, on Thursdays. Many inmates come to the meetings, some with years of experience in AA. While some of the men who attend the meetings are very familiar with AA, many of those I talk with struggle with the idea of spiritual living. It seems beyond their grasp, far too complicated, or elusive.

I love those meetings and the incarcerated men who attend them. I am certainly no authority on spiritual matters, but it is my hope that sharing my experiences as a fellow alcoholic will motivate them to continue their spiritual growth. Some inmates have developed an extraordinary attachment to their God and to spiritual living and truly lead exemplary lives. Other inmates seem to shy away from the belief that spiritual living is available to them, that God as they know Him has any interest in their lives. AA meetings offer the hope that God does care for them and that their lives, even while they are incarcerated, are valuable to God.

Many times the volunteers at the meetings will give their story, some of them very impressive. Those who have been incarcerated themselves can speak more directly to the inmates than I can. My story isn't too dramatic. I was kind of a candy-ass drunk, and I am not too sure how much good my story would be to men in prison. Certainly I am an alcoholic. I did the dumbest things, but I was lucky to avoid legal trouble. I, like most alcoholics, drove during blackouts, and it is only by the grace of God that I was never caught and never killed myself or another.

Rather than tell my less-than-dramatic story, I decided to spend my time with the inmates trying to break down the Steps in a way they would remember and then help them come to believe that a spiritual awakening was available to them, just as it is to alcoholics in the free world. Maybe learning the Steps is more important to those imprisoned because they have a more immediate need for peace and serenity than those of us who have other life distractions. The Steps show us the way to live outside ourselves, seek the will of God, and they show us how to get the power to carry out His will.

There is a difference between meetings in jail and those in prison. When a person is initially arrested, he or she is taken to jail, where he or she stays until the case is adjudicated. When people come into the jail, many of them are drunk or high on one drug or another. Frequently they are combative and hostile, and in the worst cases, they are strapped to a metal chair and put in what I call "time out." Their behavior ranges from violently ugly to disgusting to pathetic. Only after they have been incarcerated for a period of time can they request to attend AA meetings, and then it is at the jailer's discretion whether to let them attend.

Inmates who come to meetings in jail are, for the most part, very motivated but distracted. They are like cats on a hot tin roof because they are concentrating on who their lawyer is, when their court date will be, and what their final punishment will be. Unlike the men who are in prison who already know their fate, it is difficult for those in jail to focus on something for the long-term. While it is not my job to question their motivation, I admire and respect their willingness to hear and learn. I respect their courage to ask for help. Attending the meetings takes some guts, as well as an admission their addictions are ruining their lives.

Frequently when inmates are called out for the meeting in jail, the real buttheads, those who think they are cool and sophisticated jail folks, will call out, "Quitter." They laugh at those looking into or participating in AA meetings. "There go the quitters," they say. So I thank the guys who attend and appreciate that they are reaching out for a better way of life where they will have a chance to live in God's light and stop the terror they create in their families and society when they are acting out under the lash of their addictions. Thank you, quitters; keep coming to meetings. We love to have you there. I quit in 1985 and got to go home after my AA meetings. Chances are that the "quitters" will see the light of day outside the jail walls long before the jeerers.

Life in prison is significantly different from life in jail. When one goes behind the gates of a prison and realizes that he or she may not be getting out for five, ten, or fifteen years or more, frustration and a sense of helplessness kicks in forcefully. Without help, many fall into despair. Many of the incarcerated regret the mess they made out of their lives. They regret that they are incarcerated and that they are separated from their families. The list of regrets can go on and on. The resulting despair can drag them into depression, and they constantly face the reality of giving up on life.

Prison is, for the most part, an awful place. It is noisy, tough, and cold, and if it were not for AA and the many religious groups working and volunteering, I don't know how many could survive its rigors. I know I couldn't. Most prisons are severely overcrowded and a large percentage of the population is made up of addicts and/or mentally ill individuals. The noise is continuous, the smells horrendous and, with the exception of the time spent in AA or other recovery meetings, there is no place where one can find peace and quiet. I know no group that needs serenity more than the men and women behind bars. The good news is when these prisoners accept the reality of a Higher Power, they can accept the gift of serenity that comes from knowing they have a God who loves them no matter where they are. Some of the freest men I know have fifteen or twenty more years to serve, but they are free in their souls because God has become their constant companion. Some of the prisoners truly do change and are, beyond doubt, friends of God. The reformation is amazing.

I remember vividly an AA meeting at the Wynne Unit in Huntsville, Texas. One of the attendees was expressing his frustration about prison life and said, "There is nothing here that we have control over. The man tells us what to do, when to do it, and when to stop doing it. There is no freedom in here." I shot back, "That is not true. You can control what you think about and what you focus on. You can pray, and you can think about something better than "the man." You can focus your attention on something positive."

He said nothing, and I thought I had made him mad; he looked at me as if I were from Mars. After the meeting, he came up to me, gave me the biggest bear hug he could, and said, "You inspire me." I am humbled at his response and humbly hope that maybe these words can inspire someone else.

None of us wants to minimize their offences, and we have no interest in justifying the inmates' past actions. We do want to convince them that life is not over—that life, even behind bars, is worthwhile and that these men and women are meaningful to God. All of us can, and do, have moments of frustration and despair. That is normal. A healthy person can overcome those feelings of despair. But for many behind bars, those feelings are confirmed by the reality that they are locked up with some tough characters. A spiritual way of living may be the furthest thing from their minds, but might be the best way to survive whatever sentence they have to serve.

There is one old boy in Huntsville, a lifer, who is a walking example of the power of God's grace found in the AA program. This man carries his *Big Book* and Bible with him wherever he goes. He rose above the crap that goes on around him every day and has truly found an inner peace that allows him to live in real serenity. His mind and soul are not in prison. He loves AA and his God and is always smiling and helpful at meetings and elsewhere.

For most prisoners, the temptation to give up on life is real. However, this gentleman has overcome that temptation. He has overcome the normal reaction to the guilt and shame felt by many inmates. Many who try to live without help accept that they have ruined their entire lives; they are screw-ups, failures, and losers who have to suffer the consequences of their actions. Suffer the consequences? Yes. But give up on life? No. This man is a walking example of the power of God's grace that can be found in the AA program, and thankfully, there are many just like him.

There is nothing anyone has done that can't be forgiven by God. Sometimes we forget that truth. With the help of God, AA, and the Steps, lives do change. Amends can be made, redemption is possible, and freedom from drugs and alcohol becomes commonplace. As inmates begin to grow spiritually, they take ownership of their actions, past and present. They learn that to keep recovery, they need to do what they can to pass it on to others. They, just like the rest of us in the program, need to give it away in order to keep it. They pass it on by helping each other, by encouraging their fellow inmates to attend the meetings, and by sponsoring the next inmate seeking recovery through AA.

Most of the men I have met in the meetings at the Huntsville prison have a strong interest in understanding a spiritual way of living. Keep in mind, the people who attend the AA meetings are truly interested in reforming their lives. They hear on a regular basis that they should change and turn their lives around. They hear a consistent message from counselors, chaplains, and motivational speakers. While many of them find their answers in religion, the addict behind bars faces the same dilemma as those of us outside the walls. For most of us, church and religion don't work until we get sober. Many of us do believe in God and attend a church. We pray for sobriety, but we still don't succeed. Our religions teach us we should live a life of sobriety, but don't teach us how to do that.

For addicts, words and teachings are not sufficient because we don't believe sobriety is possible. Like Doubting Thomas, we need someone to show us. AA teaches us how to live and then shows us how to be restored to sanity. When the mind is open and willing and the body is free of chemicals, the soul can understand spiritual teachings. This is true. I know an inmate who was a minister on the outside and still ministers behind the walls. He often tells me that while his religion taught him about God, AA showed him how to have a life-changing relationship with God.

The folks behind bars, just like the rest of us in AA, come to the realization that life changes are necessary if they want to overcome their addictions. Those who are serious about sobriety will come to realize that the necessary changes have to start while they are still in jail or prison. If serious about changing, none of us can wait for that "perfect" day to start the change. A prisoner can't wait until the day he is free, a mom can't wait until her first child is in kindergarten, and a businessman can't wait until that next big deal is done. The longer-term inmates often tell the new guys, "Take on the program now. Begin to find the person from whom you will no longer have to run. If you are a fool inside the gates unless you make the necessary changes, you will still be a fool outside the gates of prison."

One prisoner attended our AA meeting in jail for weeks on end. He, like most in jail, was waiting to hear the timing and results of his trial for his sixth DUI. While he was waiting, he attended and was active at, AA meetings. When he got his sentence, twenty years, all of a sudden he didn't need the meetings any more. When his attendance didn't serve to influence the judge to shorten his sentence, he had no need to join the group on Tuesday nights. Changing was no longer important to him. Hopefully he will come back to the meetings. He will learn that AA members don't shoot their wounded. They will welcome him back with open arms.

Unfortunately, alcoholics and addicts can understand his way of thinking and acting. He had given up on himself and his opportunity for sobriety. He had reached the "oh screw it" place. The "oh screw it" place is that place where we give up any hope for improvement or change. We think, "Nothing will ever be right. What's the sense of putting in the effort if it's not going to make any difference anyway?" This man who quit attending meetings would rather feel sorry for himself than change. He faces the probability of spending the next twenty years fighting the system, himself, and everyone around him.

AA rarely works for those who are attending meetings and attempting the Steps in order to convince someone else that they have changed. The change cannot be because someone else wishes it—warden or wife. AA works when you know in your gut that you have to change for yourself, your sanity and perhaps your life.

If you are blessed enough to be a former inmate who survived prison with the support of AA, I hope you will consider being a messenger to take the AA program back behind bars. I was sober and in AA for twenty years before I had the opportunity to participate in prison meetings. One of my old buddies, whom I have known for twenty-five years, told me that my attendance at the AA prison meetings has changed me. He is right. Yes, it takes time, and I do have to drive forty miles each way and blah, blah, blah, but I have received more than I have ever given. I have met some wonderful men who desire what AA has to offer. They lift me up more than I can lift them. Sure, there are disappointments; there are the con men who will try to take advantage of you, but so be it. We are doing God's work in AA, and He doesn't get conned.

The AA experience behind bars is the same as in the free world. It's the same program for people with the same problems. Free or imprisoned, an alcoholic is an alcoholic. We each need God, and we alcoholics can find Him through the Twelve Steps laid down by the founders of AA.

The following poem was written by one of the members of Last Man Standing in the Wynne Unit, Huntsville, Texas. The poem is printed as it was written. It illustrates the frustration that prisoners deal with on a daily basis.

A Mental Prison
By Raul M.

There are prisons that take away a person's freedom
Controlling criminal activity is why we need 'em

Then there are prisons of a mental kind
Which incarcerates a person's mind.

Physical prisons take away the ability to function in society
Removing possessions and everything taken lightly.

Most often it's the things taken for granted that mean so much
Hoping to have money sent or for loved ones to keep in touch.

Wishing for a visit, but on one will come and stop by
Writing letters to any and everyone but getting no reply.

The mail call comes and then it's gone
And I really start to wonder, am I ever going home?

Did I have a shot at life or was I just fooling myself?
And now, here I sit, chillin', alone—with no one else.

The only thing left to do is make the best of a bad situation
Many sleepless nights worried with anxiety and anticipation.

Baby's momma got married with another kid,
thought to teach me a lesson
Why did I have to go fire that .357?

Telling and retelling my stories while secretly wishin' and hopin'
To fix or repair everything I had broken.

Last thing on my mind before I go to sleep,
the first when I wake up each day
Wondering how everyone is doing and if my child is okay.

Maurice C.

Knowing nothing about my son due to incarceration
I've longed to be a father to my most wonderful creation.

Just needing somebody, anybody to say that everything is all right
Waiting for mail that'll never come and keep asking,
"Why don't they write?"

Dealing with those who treat me harsh and unkind
Making it that much worse while trying to do my time.

Not wanting to borrow anything for fear of not being able
to pay it back
Can't finish watching the rest of a good movie or show
because of the 10:30 p.m. rack.

Half of the people snore so loud that it keeps me awake every night
Bad enough that my cell is flooded with this big-ol' bright light.

Angry and irritable because there won't be any rest for sure now
In thirty more minutes, I'll hear, "Get ready for chow!"

Praying that I won't get hassled on the way
And not catch a case because the "boss-man" is having a bad day.

That's when it's most important to consider the consequences
of my action(s)
Decide it's not worth it and don't give 'em the satisfaction(s).

Changing my thinking and thought-pattern can change how I react
Breaking free of that mental prison and getting my life back on track.

Christianity and Alcoholics Anonymous

Our world has a certain understanding of what makes sense. It makes sense to work hard to get ahead. It makes sense to practice in order to perfect a skill. It makes sense to take charge of our lives. It makes sense to be practical, crafty, shrewd, self-promoting, the leader, and in charge and acquire money, power, and prestige.

What makes sense in God's world doesn't necessarily make sense in ours. God tells us we must surrender in order to win. He tells us that by helping others, we help ourselves. He tells us that to receive all, we have to be humble. Nobody in our world ever won a war by surrendering. We are taught to think of ourselves as, and watch out for, number one. As alcoholics, we could never understand how helping others helps us even more than those we help. It makes no human sense to be humble. The world requires we toot our own horn as much and as loud as possible. God doesn't have a horn. It makes perfect worldly sense to build our fortune and reputation as much as possible. God asks us to give to the needy and shun the first place. The man seeking a spiritual life moves from the sensible material world to the nonsense world of God's values.

As I have said before, church and my religion were, and still are, very important to me. When I was introduced to AA, I had a real fear that AA's teachings might contradict what I firmly believed as part of my Christian faith. If you are a non-Christian or a non-believer, you may have the opposite fear—that AA will try to force you into one faith or another. Neither is true.

One thing that bothers me at some AA meetings is the reluctance of the members to name their God, especially if His name is Christ. If someone quotes Buddha or the Koran, most people don't take note. But if one mentions Christ or the Bible, there may be some objection as to the political correctness of that religion. Even at some AA meetings we go for political correctness, no matter what. We can get so politically correct that words lose their meaning. I ask you to keep an open mind about what I have to say in this chapter or put the book down. This chapter is for those of you not offended by reading *my* religious views. The last thing I want to do is scare anyone away from recovery from any addiction. The following thoughts, while I believe they complement the Twelve Steps, are *not* part of any AA literature. I do want to share them because in the life of Christ we see the perfect example of a life led in accordance with God's will and the perfect example of getting out of self by doing for others. Even if you are a non-believer, you can use the story of His life to better understand true humility.

Remember back to my syllogism, poorly crafted as it was. Recall that I equated God to humility. If you look into the written Word of God, the Old and New Testaments, it is hard to always see God as humility in the Old Testament, but humility is all He is in the New Testament. There is not one act reported by the authors of the gospels in which Christ does anything that is self-serving. He lived to serve men and do the will of the Father.

Jesus, through whom all things were created, was born to a teenage girl—a virgin of no fame or fortune. Mary was approached by an angel who told her she was to have a baby and that the baby's name would be Jesus. Mary said yes to God's plan and conceived by an act of the Spirit. Her husband-to-be, a local carpenter, had no idea what was going on and only took Mary for his wife when the angel appeared again and told him to do so. Mary and Joseph surely had other plans for their lives, yet they followed God's will for them and said yes to His request.

The gospel stories tell us that Joseph, along with all Jews in Israel, was directed by the ruling Roman government to take his family to his place of birth so they could be properly counted in the census. Joseph took his pregnant wife to Bethlehem. The child was born in Bethlehem, not in a home or proper place, but in a stable, and his first visitors were local shepherds, not family and friends. He could have been born a wealthy prince in a fine palace, surrounded by servants and every earthly comfort. In fact, this is what the Jews expected—an earthly king who would become a warrior and overthrow the Roman government. Instead He chose to come in humility as a weak infant. I have nothing against the people who didn't recognize Him; my guess is that if we had been there, we might not have recognized Him either.

We know little of Jesus's boyhood besides being told in Luke, chapter two, verse 40, that He "grew in wisdom and stature." He was raised as any Jewish son of a carpenter would be raised. The only story of Jesus as a youth tells of when He went with His family to worship at the temple in Jerusalem. Mary, Joseph, and the family left Jerusalem, assuming that Jesus was traveling with other family members in the group. Several hours went by before they realized Jesus was not with them, and they had to turn and walk all the way back to Jerusalem to find Jesus. They found Him at the temple, talking with "great authority" to the temple priests and elders. When Mary asked Him what He was doing (let us guess that she was more than a little put out by being scared to death that she had lost her son and having to waste several hours walking), Jesus asked her if she did not want Him to be about His Father's business.

He disappeared from written history for the most part until, as an adult, His mother asked Him to perform a miracle at a wedding feast. (Maybe He was Irish. He lived at home with His mother until he was thirty and did what she asked!) He started His ministry and selected some followers to join Him. Eventually one of them would betray Him and another would deny even knowing Him. His entire ministry was devoted to teaching, admonishing, and healing. He loved children, fed people who were hungry, and had compassion on a dad whose daughter had died and sisters whose brother had died. Toward the end of His ministry, this man, the Son of God, knelt on the floor, tied a towel around His waist, and taking a task reserved for servants, washed the dirty, dusty, feet of His disciples. This was an act of true humility.

At the end of His days, He was condemned to death, scourged, spat upon, forced to carry a crude wooden cross some distance, and nailed to a cross. He never spoke one word of resistance. He never asked, "Don't you know who I am?" He could have commanded legions of angels to free Him and destroy His enemies, but He chose death. Included in His last words were, "Father, forgive them, for they know not what they do." Jesus demonstrated total submission to the will of the Father and chose to lay down His life so His children, His own creation, could be reunited with the Father. He achieved that goal by giving up His own will for that of the Father. We achieve our goal of sobriety by turning our will and life over to the care of that same Father.

Many of us in AA wonder if God can ever truly forgive us. We have done some awful things, hurt many people, and may have broken all ten of the Ten Commandments. How could God forgive what we have done? Look at the people surrounding Jesus at His death. Peter denied he even knew Jesus, yet Jesus said that Peter was the rock upon which He would build His church. The last man to talk to Jesus before He died was a thief. He asked Jesus to save him, and Jesus replied that He would see the man in Paradise that day. There is nothing we have done that is unforgivable if we have the humility to ask. Read again the words of Jesus in Luke, chapter 23, verse 34, asking God to forgive the very people who had pounded nails through His hands and feet. If He could forgive those, do not doubt that He will also forgive you.

Before finding AA, I would say that I knew my religion very well, but I never crossed the line of turning belief into living. I did believe in an almighty God who helped people—other people. I was either too good or too bad for Him to be active in my life, or so I thought. I went through life as if I were the source of all the good I had and had an unspoken and unrealized sense that I didn't need God. He used His grace on folks who were needier than I was. I had a good job, good life, good family, and good wife, and I earned it all. During the first days of my introduction to AA, I feared there would be conflict between what AA taught and what my church taught.

In a matter of weeks, after some experience with meetings, the literature, and most importantly the people in AA, I realized these men and women were doing what my religion taught. They were living the message of Christ in a way I could see and understand, even though some of them were not Christians. For me, the spiritual life had been a theory; for the AA members, the Steps were and are a way of living Christ's message of love and service. The alcoholics in recovery sought the same spiritual path as Christ. They didn't just talk about service to their fellow man; they lived it. They made efforts to rid themselves of selfishness, the root of the problem for both the Christian and the drunk.

As I progressed through the Steps with my sponsor, Henry, I was actually doing what my religion taught. I admitted I was powerless and needed God's help. I came to believe that God could work in my life because He worked in the lives of my fellow AAs. I turned my will and life over to His care once I knew what they were. I did the moral inventory and made my confession, and in a real way, I took ownership of my misdeeds. There was no longer a need to justify why I did what I did. I took ownership of my actions, maybe for the first time in my life. I came to the point where I didn't want anything to stand in the way of my relationship with my God and Savior.

The founders of AA encouraged those of us so inclined to seek out religion. For those of us who embrace Christianity as well as AA, we have a double-barreled shotgun; one enhances the other. As one of my buddies in Huntsville Prison said, "My religion tells me what to do, and AA shows me how to do it." As a young man, I had the idea that I had to do good. I had to be faithful, honest, pure, etc. I know now, after many years of failure at doing it on my own, it is only with God's grace that I can do all the things I was taught by my church, my parents, and the Boy Scouts. (I was ejected from the Boy Scouts.) My faith strengthens my AA and AA enhances my faith. I am doubly blessed.

Final Thoughts

Frequently in AA meetings we hear people ask, "How does AA work?" Well, now you know how I think it works. It works because we have reached the point of desperation and realize that we either get help or we die. It works by teaching us that we can't do it by ourselves, but we can do it with the help of God and our fellow AA members. It works because we can finally begin to take down the defensive walls we have been hiding behind. It works because we have finally admitted our faults and taken Steps to amend the harm we have done to others. Our lives change because we stop trying to be the center of the universe and just let God do His job. We stay ready to be His messenger to other alcoholics.

I hope in some way the exercise of reading this book has led you to a deeper understanding of the spirituality of Alcoholics Anonymous. Those of us who are members of the fellowship are lucky and blessed. Years ago, if I heard someone say, "God bless you," I thought it was a nice thing to say, but really meant "good luck." Today, I know it's a prayer. It's a prayer for you so may God bless you. I hope when someone says that to you, your response can be, "He has." If you are a sober alcoholic today, you are blessed and highly favored.

One of the men I sponsored, Frank M., passed away in 1990. He left me this poem, which he always wanted to have published. I thank Frank for the trust he placed in me as his sponsor. He would be thrilled to see his work in print.

Run with the Wind like a Deer
By Frank M.

I had nothing to give, though I wanted to
For to give is to set myself free,
Funny thing is, if I'm honest;
I've gone back to just thinking of me.

Why is it so hard to see things?
Why is it so hard to hear?
Why is it so hard,
To allow God to let me
Run with the wind like a deer?

So maybe I do have a gift I can give,
Maybe I've something to share.
If I can just keep trying,
I'll learn how to listen.
If I can just keep trying,
I'll learn how to hear.

Someday I can tell you just how it is,
To run with God and the wind,
Like a deer!

God bless you! Hope to see you at a meeting.

.

9 781449 726232